In Memory of
My Mom and Dad,

Bessie Todecheenie
and
Jerald Mac Tanner

Dedicated to

My 9 children,

28 grandchildren,

and 5 great-grandchildren as of this writing.

History molds the person:
this is mine, and it is theirs.

Table of Contents

Prologue

If you google the term half-breed you will find that it is considered an offensive term. The Merriam Webster dictionary defines half-breed as the offspring of parents of different races, especially the offspring of an American Indian and a white person. As a child of the 1950s and '60s, growing up on the Navajo reservation, I often heard the term and was unaware of its meaning until I got older. As I'm sure you can imagine, life on the reservation during my childhood was quite different from the modern reservation of today. According to the Bureau of Indian Affairs, the Navajo population in 1955 was about 77,200 and like most traditional Navajo families, I lived in a matriarchal community that was isolated by clan and the vastness of the reservation.

As I grew older, I began to realize that I looked different from other Navajo children and the excitement of going to school was replaced with sadness and confusion due to the cruel teasing from classmates. "Hey, *bilagáana*" (white person) I often heard, and half-breed is what I was called. Yes, it was offensive, and yes, it hurt me deeply. Unfortunately, this is part of our country's history, part of Native history and it is part of my history, and so my book is titled *Half-Breed*.

When Clare, my co-author, and I first talked about writing a book about my life, I was excited and nervous at the same time because I had no idea how to go about it. He assured me that together we could do it; he had written two books previously so knew the process. With lots of encouragement Clare said all I had to do was tell my stories and find the pictures to go with them, and so four or five years ago we started researching and documenting my life events.

You could say that my life has had a lot of twists and turns, some planned and some unexpected. Add to that being a mixed-race child during the '50s and '60s on a mostly homogeneous reservation did not prepare me for what was to come. The first few years of my life I was insulated from the unkind world that I would later experience. My mom, sister, and grandma—the matriarchs of the family—were always there to love me unconditionally, guide me with our traditions, and provide me with affection and advice when I needed it.

My journey has taken me on and off the reservation several times throughout my life. I am no different, I have experienced success, fallen a time or two, and have felt heartache and joy. I have finally settled in Phoenix and enjoy my life here, but there will always be that pull back to the reservation where I was born and where a piece of my heart will always be.

Many times, as we have been writing this book, I have asked myself, *Why didn't you ask that question when you could?* But I didn't, and now I find myself the most senior member of my family. So, there is no one to ask.

As a Navajo, I belong to the largest Native American tribe in the United States, with currently nearly 400,000 tribal members and the largest reservation that is over 27,000 square miles and extends into the states of Arizona, New Mexico and Utah. I am blessed to be here, as our population was once greatly diminished.

My ancestors were determined to live and return to their homeland. I admire their strength and resilience to continue and pass down our traditions. Let me properly introduce myself. My name is Verna. I am *Kinłichii'nii* (Red House clan), born for *Bilagáana* (white people). My maternal grandfather is *Tódich'ii'nii* (Bitter Water clan). My paternal grandfather is *Bilagáana* (white people). This is how I identify myself as a Navajo woman.

After you have read my book, I hope you will know more about my people, the Navajo. I am proud of who I am and I'm excited to share my story with you. Writing it has been soul searching, but fun.

I hope you enjoy the book.

Verna Begay

Note: American Indian and Native American will be used interchangeably throughout the book. References for my prologue can be found in the bibliography.

CHAPTER 1

Growing up on the Navajo Reservation

It seemed like a long time ago since she had first carded the wool, straightening the wool fibers one handful at a time so they could be spun into strands of yarn. Three times she had spun the wool, first into a bulky strand, then into the size she wanted, and then a final time to perfect the size into a uniform ball of yarn. She had boiled the sunflowers to make the yellow dye, the walnuts to make a tan dye and the cactus bugs to make red. She had then soaked and simmered the yarn she had prepared in the dye solutions and hung the yarn up to dry after the desired color had been achieved.

Once the yarn was dry, she started weaving on the loom she had fashioned from pieces of wood, keeping a close watch that each of the geometric designs would be perfect. And now it was done and she was excited to take it to Sunrise Trading Post to sell or trade for things at the trading post that she wanted and needed for herself and her young daughter. The

Sunrise Trading Post ruins.

Gallup brick.

traders there had given her credit from time to time for supplies she needed and now that must first be paid off and hopefully get some things in addition.

The Sunrise Trading Post, now just a broken-down shell along the highway, a pile of the Gallup bricks of which it was at least partially constructed, was located at Sunrise which is south of Cornfields, both being smaller communities in the vicinity of Ganado, a larger community and all on the Navajo Reservation in Arizona. In its heyday the trading post included living quarters for the traders, a building for storage of hay, grain and other commodities and a corral for livestock, At least that is what my memory is telling me.

The trading post was run by white traders who would barter with Navajo artists for their artwork or other commodities in exchange for things they had to offer for sale. She had gone there with her parents, my grandpa and grandma, since my grandma also made Navajo rugs, several times before, so she knew how it was done.

She was now on her own, her husband having passed away, and she had a daughter to care for and she needed things for herself and her daughter. So off with her horse and wagon she went to negotiate the sale of her rug. As the handsome white trader who was married to his three-months pregnant wife, and this young beautiful Navajo widow, who had a young daughter, negotiated, sparks started to fly and in an afternoon of passion, which my mother never spoke about, at least to me, until the truth was revealed, I was conceived. My white brother was born at Sage Memorial Hospital in Ganado, while less than six months later I was born at my grandma's hogan. Did my mother and father have some sort of a relationship other than the day I was conceived? Probably, although I am only guessing.

The handsome white trader (Verna's Dad) at work showing a Navajo rug.

I am Navajo. I was born Navajo. I was raised Navajo and I speak the Navajo language. And so, when the social studies teacher at Intermountain Indian School was explaining how Christopher Columbus had discovered America, I raised my hand and the teacher called on me. "We were here a long time before Columbus came here," I said. I knew I was right. My grandma had told me about how our ancestors came to this area and settled a long time ago, in the area now called the Colorado Plateau that radiates out from the Four Corners area of Arizona, New Mexico, Utah and Colorado. Our ancestors arrived here probably between 200 and 1300 A.D. Columbus didn't arrive until 1491. I can't remember how the teacher responded to being corrected, but I knew I was right.

The teacher had one story and I had a different story. As I have learned since that encounter at Intermountain, here is the real story. In 1452, Catholic Pope Nicholas V released a papal bull, an order that authorized the Christian nations to establish ownership to any lands that they encountered or discovered that were not already inhabited and claimed by other

Christian rulers, and to take possession of the land, and property, and non-Christian inhabitants, heathens, of that land. Columbus had convinced Ferdinand II and Isabella I, rulers of Spain, to finance his voyage. He was really looking for a route by water to the orient, to India, that could be used for the spice trade, and while others had attempted that feat by sailing east, Columbus thought he could find a water route to the orient by sailing west. When he finally reached land, he planted the flag of Spain signifying ownership for Spain as he had agreed to do. Columbus didn't discover America, as students were being taught, but he did establish a pathway for future voyages that would result in tragic results for tribes across America and eventually to the country we now have and enjoy. That journey is a story for another day.

Childhood on the Navajo Reservation was carefree. Much of our time was spent playing outdoors except during bad weather, without the constant supervision that is necessary today, finding pictures in the clouds on a scattered cloudy day or counting the airplanes, especially the jets with vapor trails. We could gallop around on our pretend horse that was simply a tree branch. Or drive down the road in our pretend car formed by nailing a can lid to a tree to make the pretend steering wheel. Or build houses or hogans by lining up rocks or sticks to form the outline of a house or hogan on the ground.

My grandma owned some horses and sheep. At grandmas we had fun playing around the horses, with no fear of running underneath them: the horses seemed to know. Or making friends with the sheep or with the dogs and cats. In order to pass the time in winter or bad weather, my big sis Jessie and I would spent hours playing ball and jacks or marbles or finger string games making different designs.

Memories of butchering a sheep or goat for food was an exciting time because it usually was along with a feast or ceremony of some kind but also a sad time. At first, I would cry when a sheep was killed, but then I would watch as the blood was collected in a bowl in preparation for adding potatoes to make blood sausage. I would watch as the head was removed and put in the fire to burn off the wool and skin. The skin of the sheep was then skillfully removed from the carcass to become a sheepskin for clothing or a bedroll or for some purpose such as trading at the trading post. I would grimace as the vertebrae at the back of the skull was chopped off and the head was passed around so each person there could reach into the skull with one or two fingers and pull out some cooked brain to be licked off their fingers. Yes, I have eaten cooked sheep brains.

I watched with interest as the omentum was removed and hung up for later use, and I grimaced as the intestines were cleaned and prepared for consumption later. Nothing went to waste. Bigger pieces of meat would be removed for further processing. In summer the pieces of meat would be cut in thin strips and hung to dry, sort of like jerky. The dried meat could then later be boiled along with vegetables to make a delicious stew.

Sometimes, a deep hole in the earth was dug and the wrapped meat would be buried in the cool earth for future use, or sometimes it was salted to aid in preservation. In winter, the meat would be kept in a container and frozen outside the house, always being mindful of hungry animals picking up the scent of meat. The remainder of the carcass would then be roasted over the fire and consumed either that day or over the next few days.

Another lasting memory is of a chicken being killed in preparation for a chicken dinner. When the head was chopped off, the chicken would jump all over the yard spurting blood here and there before it finally died. Scary for a young child.

As children we would look forward to Christmas time at the Presbyterian church in Cornfields. Little did we know that the church was part of a Presbyterian mission whose purpose was to convert us "heathens" to Christianity. At Christmas time each child would be given a cloth bag that had been filled with candy and toys and that was tied shut to prolong the suspense.

One Sunday morning at the Presbyterian church, the service was interrupted because a snake had slithered into the sanctuary through a small hole in the wall. As I remember, a man wearing a glove, pulled the snake out of the hole and took it outside, and the service continued. That Presbyterian

Church in Cornfields no longer exists. I am not sure if the building is still there or not, but it holds many memories for me.

Encounters with snakes were not uncommon on the reservation. I remember one time when we discovered that a snake had swallowed one of our newborn kittens. Even though Grandma had told us never to kill a snake because if you did more would come looking for it, my brother Wilbert chopped up the snake, getting revenge for eating one of our kittens.

On another occasion, when I was a little older, I was on my way to the outhouse and felt something attack my boot. I was able to get my foot on the snake's head and was amazed at how strong it was in its attempt to get away, which it did when I released its head.

Another close encounter was one day when I was herding sheep and jumped over what I thought was a pile of horse manure, but looking closer discovered that I had jumped over a coiled rattlesnake about to strike.

Grandma had told us about an experience she'd had with someone being bitten by a rattler, and how the strike was cut with a knife in the form of an x so the venom could be sucked out. Needless to say, I have no love for snakes.

Horned toad.

Unlike snakes, the horned toad holds a special place in the lives of Navajo children. We would call the toads *Cheii* which means maternal grandpa and when we scurried to catch the toad it signified playing with grandpa. Once we caught the toad, it would be held to our chest, like grandma had taught us. She said this would transfer the protection of the arrowheads and other weapons of protection on the toad's body to protect us.

Like many of the Navajo traditions, this one comes from the creation story in which the Brothers had by disobeying their mothers, Changing Woman and White Shell Woman, aroused the monsters. As the Brothers fled from the monsters, they came to the home of Spider Woman, who gave them instructions on how to avoid the hazards they would encounter on the way to visiting their father, the Sun.

Following Spider Woman's instructions, they arrived at the home of their father, the Sun, only to be told that he did not believe they were his sons. They finally convinced the Sun that he was in fact their father and the Sun gave them the weapons they would need to kill the monsters that pursued them. The arrowheads that cover the body of the horned toad represent the weapons that the Sun gave to the Brothers and tradition says that when a child holds the toad to his or her chest, the protection of the arrowheads is transferred to that child. This tradition, like many others, holds a special place in Navajo tradition and is sometimes used in ceremonies. I fondly remember encounters with horned toads growing up on the Navajo reservation.

As a young child, I spent a lot of time with Grandma Louise Todecheenie at her hogan. We had no running water on the reservation, so our water had to be carried from a community well to the hogan or house. One of the wells at Cornfields was an open well, so water would be brought to the surface with a bucket on a rope. Some wells had pumps that let you pump the water you needed by hand, and some had windmills that made pumping easier

We used barrels to haul the water back home, so we went to the well with a wagon drawn by a team of horses. (See pictures on page 8) This was a fun journey for us kids, but it was just part of the day's work for my mother or whoever went on the water mission. Water was a precious commodity on the reservation, just as it is everywhere in the southwest.

I remember going with Grandma to the wash (The Little Colorado River Wash) after a rain or snow melt, so she could wash cloths in the stream of water using a rock as a washboard. In those days, the wash would flow regularly from bountiful snowfall and rain in the mountains, and the corn would grow tall.

Little Colorado River Wash — no water for washing clothes today.

Left, typical Navajo hogan in winter.

Center, water well with hand pump equipped to fill water barrels.

Bottom, water well with a windmill.

Grandma was a skilled midwife and families would come from all around to ask her to help with the delivery of a baby. Grandma had a reputation for knowing how to skillfully redirect a baby from a breech presentation to being born head first. That put her in special demand and it was not unusual to have someone knock on the door in the middle of the night and my Grandma would drop everything and rush to their aid.

On one occasion, us kids were hustled out of the hogan to play outside. What was happening we didn't know but before long we heard screams coming from the hogan. One of the kids, me, scrapped a small hole in the dried mud between the logs so we could peek in. My Aunt was standing in the hogan holding on to a rope [a drag rope] that was tied to the roof of the hogan. Every little while she would let out a scream. But we soon lost interest and when we were allowed back in the hogan, my Aunt was holding my new cousin in her arms.

My Grandma's hogan was a traditional hogan built with logs in a circular fashion and chinked with mud. As was traditional, Grandma's hogan had a door on the east in order to catch the warmth of the morning sun. In the center was a fire pit that was used for both warmth and cooking. The smoke from the fire left the hogan through a hole in the center of the roof for that purpose. In summer the cooking was done on an outdoor fire pit.

Grandma's hogan was cozy with a dirt floor and blankets and sheepskins rolled up for use at night and piled by the wall during the day. Cozy especially on cold winter nights when we would get wrapped in the blankets and sheepskins. In the morning we would roll up our sleeping roll and store it along the wall of the hogan. Grandma had no furniture in the hogan except for a washstand inside the door with an enamelware basin and a pail of water for washing as you entered the hogan. A towel hung on a rod beside the washstand.

Our meals were served on the dirt floor of the hogan in the beginning, but after a while, as I recall, we had something like an oil cloth that would be spread out for meals. Even later I remember a table of sorts: a table top with legs four or five inches long, on which the meal would be served as we sat on the ground around it. Grandma did not have a table as we think of them today, until she had a house instead of a hogan. The dish to be served would be set on the ground or on the makeshift table and we would gather in a circle to eat. Kitchen utensils and silverware were sparse and I remember just dipping the stew out of the center bowl with a piece of frybread. My older sister, Jessie, Mom and I lived here with Grandma in the hogan until Mom married my stepdad.

Kerosene lamp.

Grandma had no electricity in her Hogan, so the only light we had after dark was a kerosene lamp. So, once it got dark each day, it was bedtime. But there was still time for stories; Grandma didn't need light to tell stories. In winter months, which is the only time coyote stories were to be told, she told us coyote stories and how to beware of doing things like those that got coyote in trouble. She told us how the coyote had been part of Navajo tradition from the very beginning, even during the creation story of Changing Woman. She told us if we paid attention, we could learn how to behave and what to watch out for. These were sometimes funny and sometimes scary stories. Coyote had magical powers and you never knew what coyote would do next. Grandma told us the story of Coyote and Rabbit:

One day, Coyote was out walking.
He was walking in the forest.
He saw Rabbit.
He started to chase Rabbit.
Rabbit ran in a hole.
Coyote said,
"I'll get you out of that hole,
Let me think."
Coyote sat down to think.
Now I know: "I'll get you out.
I'll get weeds.

I'll put them in the hole.
I'll set fire to them.
Then you will come out," said Coyote.
Rabbit laughed.
"No, I will not come out my cousin.
I like weeds. I'll eat the weeds."
"Do you eat milkweeds" asked Coyote.
"I'll get milkweeds."
"Yes, I like milkweeds.
I'll eat the milkweeds," said Rabbit.
"Do you eat foxtail grass," said Coyote.
"I'll get foxtail grass."
"Yes, I like foxtail grass.
I'll eat the foxtail grass," said Rabbit.
'Do you eat Rabbit Brush" said Coyote.
"I'll get Rabbit Brush," "I like Rabbit Brush best of all.
I'll eat the Rabbit Brush too," said Rabbit.
"I know," said Coyote. "Pinyon pitch."
Rabbit looked sad.
"You will kill me. I do not eat pinyon pitch," said Rabbit.
Coyote was happy.
He ran from pinyon tree to pinyon tree.
He gathered pinyon pitch.
He put the pinyon pitch in the hole.
He set the pinyon pitch on fire.
He bent low. He blew on the fire.
"Come closer," said Rabbit.
"Blow harder."
Coyote came closer.
He blew harder.
"I'm nearly dead," said Rabbit.
"Come closer.
Blow a little harder."

Coyote came closer.
He blew harder.
He shut his eyes.
He blew harder.
Rabbit turned.
He kicked hard.
The fire flew in Coyote's face.
Rabbit ran away.
He was laughing very hard.

Coyote stories to think about as we fell asleep. And we remembered to beware of a coyote crossing your path. Superstition said that if you crossed the path of the coyote, something bad would happen to you, so you had better go another way. Besides, with his magical powers the shadowy Coyote might turn himself into a skinwalker, and then who knows.

On other nights, Grandma would tell us stories about our ancestors and how they had to fight to keep control of the land that Changing Woman had said was theirs. She told us about Chief Narbona and how he had been killed and scalped by United States soldiers. How Kit Carson and his soldiers had tried to starve them off their land by killing their livestock and destroying their crops.

How one time about 1,000 Navajo warriors almost defeated the United States soldiers at Fort Defiance, but in the end, they were forced to surrender. How the United States federal government used the Army to force some 10,000 Navajo to walk from their homeland to the Bosque Redondo Reservation at Fort Sumner, and how many were not strong enough to survive the up to 400-mile journey (depending on what route they took).

And how the Navajo were confined there until President Andrew Johnson signed the Treaty of June 1, 1868 which created the Navajo Reservation. I have since learned that from time to time the United States Congress, and sometimes the President by executive order, enlarged the Navajo Indian Reservation to essentially what it is today.

Grandma told us about how in the mid-1930s, under President Franklin D. Roosevelt, the federal government decided, probably correctly, that the Navajo had too many sheep and goats and that they were destroying the grazing lands (or was it that they had too little land?). And how under the leadership of Commissioner of Indian Affairs, John Collier, federal agents were sent to the Navajo Reservation to direct the selling or shooting of sheep, goats, cattle and horses. She also told us the Navajo resented what the federal government was doing, because while the Anglo population measured wealth in dollars, the Navajo measured wealth in sheep. Sheep furnished meat, wool for weaving for rugs and clothing and sinew or tendons for thread. This action by the federal government, Grandma said, was almost as bad as the Long Walk. They called John Collier the "goat hater." We were not taught these things at the government boarding schools.

Grandpa was from Cornfields and Grandma was from Greasewood, but after they got married, they lived in Cornfields. So, my mom grew up in Cornfields. Grandma, Mom and several of my aunts made Navajo rugs which they would sell at the Sunrise Trading Post. Grandpa, Omar Todecheenie, was a quiet man, a true farmer in the sense of the Spanish phrase, *Apache de las Nabahu*, Apaches of the Cultivated Fields, a true example of Navajo.

He spent his time tending to his flock of sheep and goats, and his horses and cattle. He also spent hours planting and hoeing the tall corn that used to grow at Cornfields. At first, corn was planted with a planting stick which was essentially a stick to be used to punch a hole in the soil for the seed, but in later years I remember him having a horse drawn corn planter, probably issued by the federal government at the time the reservation was established.

I remember as a child the fun of running through the tall lush cornfields, but they no longer exist, partly because of changing climate that has resulted in less water in the wash, and partly because of changing lifestyles and getting away from providing the needs of the family from a parcel of land. Lastly, it is probably partly because without rotation of crops or replenishing the soil fertility, the soil was becoming depleted. My Grandpa died while I was fairly young, and after that, very little corn was planted on what was now Grandma's land.

When Mom married my stepdad, we lived part of the time at a house that my stepdad had near the Sunrise Trading Post while he was building a house near Grandma's hogan as tradition dictated. It was Navajo tradition for a new husband to build a house at the place where his new wife's family lived. That didn't happen fast, but as my stepdad could afford it, he built a little house of plywood and eventually got it covered with tar paper.

My stepdad was away working for long periods of time, and while he was away we would live at Cornfields. When he was home, we would go back and forth between the two houses. In the one room house that holds so many memories, we had a stove and one bed, but most of us still slept on the floor like at Grandma's.

CHAPTER 2

School Days

I was first enrolled at the public school in Ganado and would be picked up by the school bus. I liked school and making new friends, but that would be soured when some kids started calling me "white girl," "*Bilagáana*," "*Bilagáana*," they teased. I guess I knew I had a lighter complexion than most of my classmates, but I didn't know why. I tried to get darker by being in the sun, but Mom smiled and said, "That just makes you red instead of darker." I decided maybe she was right when the sunburn on my nose started to peel a few days later.

At first it made me cry when they called me "white girl" "*Bilagáana*" and then snickered, or when they accidentally on purpose bumped into me, or accidentally tried to trip me. Yes, there were a few fights, and a few kids learned how hard I could punch; I held my own. Soon I learned to ignore it, at least outwardly, and that probably helped to make me tough so I could defend myself, and maybe gave me the courage to do some of the things I did. But even with that, school was better than being at home if my stepdad was there and had been drinking. Eventually, some of those same kids who had taunted me became good friends.

I was in second grade when an incident happened that would put me in a different school. There were about fifteen kids in my class and one day someone threw an eraser across the room and our teacher saw it fly but not where it came from. She demanded that we tell her who had thrown the eraser. We knew who did it, but the culprit was also the bully of the class and no one was about to get on his bad side by snitching on him.

We stood our ground, which angered the teacher. "If you won't tell me who did it," she said, "then I will have to paddle you all." With that, she produced a board paddle, and asked us in turn to bend over and take our punishment. As some of the kids were crying as a result of the punishment, I was getting scared. I knew how much it would hurt because of my stepdad's use of the belt on us kids when he had been drinking and was unhappy with something we did. Somehow, when the teacher wasn't looking, I slipped out the door of the schoolhouse and ran.

The road from Ganado to Cornfields was not used much. It was just a dirt road and only church officials, missionaries, and a few other people who could afford a car used it. The rest of us traveled with horses or walked. I watched for approaching cars as I ran and darted off to safety behind a bush whenever I saw one. All was going well until I was a little slow in getting behind a bush and I was spotted. The car went by, slowed down and then backed up. I was scared. *What should I do?*

Typical Navajo transportation during my (Verna's) childhood.

As I was trying to decide whether to run, two nuns and a priest got out of the car. I could tell because of their dress. Having been to church at the Catholic church, I had the impression that priests and nuns were kind people. "Are you okay?" one of them asked. I was scared and very hesitant when they asked me to get in the car. Finally, they coaxed me enough that I got in the car and they proceeded to take me home. I remember that one of the nuns gave me a chocolate mint candy on the way. I was not a part of what went on behind the scene but I know that the school found out about what I had done and I was transferred to the Greasewood Boarding School.

Greasewood was originally settled as the result of a man who was looking in the desert for water for his livestock. When he discovered a clump of greasewood bushes with a pond of water in the center, Greasewood was born. With an abundance of water, the area became a settlement with farming as the major activity. Soon, missionaries arrived and a day school was started. In 1962, the Bureau of Indian Affairs established the Greasewood Boarding School, which first held classes in 1963. I was probably in one of the first classes held there. In 1995, the school became a tribally controlled grant school and is now Greasewood Springs Community School.

Greasewood was nice because we each had our own bed. I wasn't used to that, since at home we slept on the floor. Our beds were bunk beds lined up in a long dormitory, and we each had a metal locker for our belongings.

Meals were served on tables, which again was a change from home where we had no table. In earlier times the government would forbid students from speaking their native language, but at Greasewood we spoke both Navajo and English. That was easy for me because I had learned both Navajo and English from Mom while growing up at home. Grandma, though, spoke only Navajo.

Greasewood Boarding School dormitory.

This was my introduction to government boarding schools directed by the Bureau of Indian Affairs. Indian boarding schools had improved greatly from the early days, but they still deprived the child of their nurturing home and parents. I missed Mom, but when my stepdad was not away working, he was often drinking and home life was tense.

So, I was happy at the Greasewood Boarding School as long as they didn't make me eat lima beans. I hated lima beans then, and I still do. When lima beans or other vegetables were served, the dorm aides were there to make sure we ate our "healthy" vegetables. The day lima beans were served, I stealthily stuffed the lima beans into my empty milk carton. The dorm aide caught me and dumped the whole milky mess back onto my plate and insisted that I eat it. I was crying and the dorm aide was standing over me insisting I eat the mess on my plate. I don't remember how the impasse ended but I did not forget the incident.

My parents would occasionally pick me up and take me home for the weekend. When my mom and step-day came that Friday to take me home, I immediately blurted out the lima bean story. My stepdad, probably encouraged by having been drinking that day, cornered the dorm aide and gave her a piece of his mind for treating his daughter that way. Except for lima beans, the meals were pretty good at Greasewood.

I loved playing basketball at Greasewood. We had a good team on which I played in the forward position for the Greasewood Mustangs. We were passionate about winning and when we lost a game, we would have a good crying fest and promise to play harder next time.

Recess was spent outside playing on playground equipment, including swings, merry-go-round, monkey bars, teeter totter and slide. Whether we were inside or outside, we also got into games of jacks or marbles. On Sundays, we all went to church at the Catholic church nearby.

The people in charge at Greasewood insisted on uniformity in how students wore their hair. No long hair for boys; they all were given short haircuts. And all girls had their hair braided by the aides. On one occasion, when we all were released for what we called "school out" or summer vacation, we all returned to our homes with head lice, probably as a result of the

Greasewood Boarding School cafeteria, top.

The gymnasium at Greasewood Boarding School where I (Verna) played basketball, center left.

Greasewood Springs Mustangs today, center right.

Greasewood Catholic Church, bottom left.

aides using a shared hair brush while braiding our hair. Some kids had their heads shaved but my Mom was given something by the missionaries at the church to treat for the lice and so we were able to get it under control.

Maybe I was a bit of a mischievous child, or maybe it was just luck that when things happened that upset the dorm aides or the school authorities I just seemed to be in the vicinity, (at least that was my story). Like when the dorm aid, Ms. Truland (not her real name) — a dorm aid no one liked — got tangled in the thread that had been strung across the walkway so she would run into it in the dimly lit dorm while she was making her rounds. "Verna Mae Nez, come here right now!" she yelled at me. Without admitting anything, I will just say that this is how I got the reputation for being a troublemaker. But didn't she deserve it? As punishment she made us all get up in the middle of the night to scrub the hallways.

Or how about the time when she fell or almost fell because someone had smeared Vaseline on the walkway floor? Whether I was the culprit or not, I was the first to be blamed. I guess they probably had me figured out.

Quite often the dorm aides would have us line up for a count-off to make sure the right number of students were there. On two different occasions, that I have intimate knowledge of (wonder why?), the number came up short and the authorities were notified that some students were missing. The security patrol, that drove a truck or van-type vehicle we called the "gray bucket," would patrol the perimeter of the school regularly. When they got this notice, they would travel further from the school looking for the run-aways.

On one occasion that I remember, one of my friends had not done her work assignment well enough, at least in the eyes of the dorm aid, and she was ordered to redo it. She rebelled and wanted to go home to get away from this mean dorm aide. Three of us were ready to help her, so the four of us sneaked out of Greasewood Boarding School and started running toward Cornfields, which was some ten or twelve miles away.

As it was starting to get dark, we came to an empty shack where we decided to spend the night. It was spooky in that abandoned shack and we were scared. We didn't get much sleep that night and it seemed like forever before the sun started to come up. When it was light enough, we started out again. We hadn't gotten very far when the "gray bucket" appeared and we were taken back to school to face the music.

It seemed that even if I wasn't the one in trouble, I was willing to support the one who had an issue and so became as guilty as they were.

The second escape that I was a part of involved three girls. We were able to get to the home of one of my partners in crime, and

The shack where we runaways spent the night.

we had enough time to eat a good home-cooked meal before the school authorities were notified and two of us were taken back to school. The girl who initiated the escape was allowed to stay with her parents so they could have a heart-to-heart talk before she was taken back to school.

So, as I am sure you have figured out by now, I just seemed to be unlucky enough to be in the vicinity when things happened. And if you believe that…

If memory serves me right, I think I attended Greasewood Boarding School for about five years before I followed my older sister, Jessie, to Intermountain Indian School in Brigham City, Utah.

Fast-forward several years as one of my daughters prepared to go to Greasewood Boarding School. As bad luck would have it, she got Ms. Truland as her dorm aide. Sadly for her, she automatically had a bad reputation just because she was Verna Mae Nez's daughter. I enrolled my son at Greasewood Boarding School when he was old enough too, but when he was injured on the first day of school while running on the bleachers, I took him out of Greasewood and entered him in Ganado Public School so I could keep a closer eye on him. After all, he was my only son.

CHAPTER 3

Home Life on the Rez

My stepdad could be a very nice man, and that man I have to assume is the man that my mom fell in love with. But when he was drinking, which was much of the time as I remember it, he was an abusive and scary person.

He was away working for long periods of time, but on one particular winter night he was home and we were at his house near the Sunrise Trading Post. I can't remember the details, but I was probably home from Greasewood Boarding School for the weekend or it was a winter school out (vacation). Jessie was living with Grandma then, and going to Ganado Public School.

As the evening wore on and he drank more and more, my stepdad got louder and louder and more abusive towards my mom. Eventually they were arguing and that led to fighting, with my mom obviously getting the worst of the deal just because of the size and strength of my stepdad. "Stop, Daddy, you are hurting my mom!" I shouted through my tears. But he wouldn't stop. I was scared. He would often whip us kids with a belt and I feared I would be next, so out the door I ran. Never mind that it was winter.

I don't remember what I was wearing, but I remember it was cold. I was going to the safety of Grandma's hogan some six or so miles down the snow-covered road. There happened to be a full moon that night, so its light shining on the snow lit my path. I ran, and I stumbled in the snow.

I got back up and ran some more. I was determined to get to Grandma's hogan in Cornfields.

It seemed like it took forever. I guess it was pretty late, because when I finally got to my grandma's hogan, she was fast asleep. I pounded on the door until it finally opened. I was so, so cold. The fire in the hogan had died down to just some embers but Grandma got the fire going again and then started rubbing my arms and legs to get the blood circulating in my body again. In my fear, I had made a foolish decision. I could just as well have been found frozen in a snowbank the next morning. But I was there and I was safe, and Grandma would take care of me.

From Bad to Worse

In 2017, the Sexual Assault Prevention subcommittee on the Navajo reservation found that the Navajo police receive an average of six reports of rape per week with 22% of Navajo children receiving health services being seen for sexual abuse or assault. They "estimated that one-in-four Navajo children have experienced some form of sexual abuse."

Privacy in a one room Navajo house or hogan is difficult: no, it's non-existent. As a young girl growing up, I wondered why my dad would treat us like he did. But I was too young to understand what was happening. I would often see my sister Jessie crying and when I would ask her what was wrong, she would say, I hate that man! As we grew older it just didn't seem right. Jessie and I would sometimes talk about it. We were not comfortable around our dad.

Then one day my dad did something to me that changed the path that my life would take. My little brother was sick and my Mom was napping with him. Jessie was living with Grandma at that time but that day she had been there with me until she left the house to do something. I don't remember what led up to it, but my dad started touching me in a way that was not comfortable. It wasn't technically rape, I guess, but it was certainly sexual child abuse. I was young. I didn't know about such things. I was scared. I tried to get my Mom's attention but she shushed me not wanting to wake my little brother. I bolted out of the house and ran to my

Grandmas hogan. I was crying and when I told my Grandma what had happened to me, my Grandma or aunt or someone in the family, took charge. The incident was reported and an investigation of my stepdad's spousal abuse and sexual abuse was started. I don't know what the outcome was for my stepdad. Jessie and I were questioned by someone in authority: police or tribal official or social worker? I don't know. What I do remember is that I was scared; It made me feel like I was the one that had done something wrong. Why would my dad do that to me, I said? Now I knew what Jessie had been trying to tell me.

And that is when my aunt told me that my biological Dad was the white trader at Sunrise Trading Post. Not that this made it right but it made it easier to understand. But I thought I was Navajo, and I am, but now I'm also white, I'm also English, I'm also "bilagáana" just like the kids in school had teased. I wasn't sure if I was happy or sad. On top of the violence at home and the sexual abuse, this was a lot for a teenager to make sense of.

I would never go back to my Mom's house again when my stepdad was around. Jessie would escape by transferring to Intermountain Indian School and following an argument involving my Mom, my stepdad and Grandma, my Grandma prevailed and I would live with her until I too went to Intermountain.

I don't exactly remember when, but eventually my Mom and I would talk about my biological father and how when she would visit the trading post, he would hold me in his arms and look at me with that loving fatherly gaze.

The boys in the family were treated differently by my step dad than the girls, but we all lived in fear of the belt when my stepdad was drinking. He would often force my brothers to go outside with him and while he drank, they were forced to sing Navajo songs with him. Not much fun for a child, but they had no choice if they wanted to avoid the belt.

For obvious reasons, I didn't go back home from Utah for almost four years. But when I did go home to Cornfields, I enrolled at the College of Ganado where I would finish high school.

Me (Verna) in a cradle board being held by Dad at the Sunrise Trading Post. My brother, Lynn, says this is him, but this baby is way too cute to be a boy

CHAPTER 4

Home Life is Intolerable

My older sister Jessie had left home earlier to go to Intermountain Indian School, because of intolerable conditions at home, and that is where I wanted to go. I boarded a bus with other Navajo students and we rode for what seemed like forever, actually a little over 500 miles, and got to the Intermountain Indian School the next morning.

During World War II the city of Brigham City, Utah donated a parcel of land to the federal government for the establishment of a military hospital. Bushnell Army Hospital was created and served wounded soldiers from 1942 to 1946. The former hospital sat empty until 1948 when Brigham City got a proposal for establishing an Indian school. President Harry Truman signed the bill authorizing money and Intermountain Indian School was established. The school first took Navajo students in 1950. The school was a Navajo only boarding school until 1974 when it was opened to all tribes. In 1984 the school was closed and the property deeded back to the city of Brigham City.

Intermountain was set up different than Greasewood. One of the buildings had a dormitory but where I was had rooms with four students to a room with two sets of bunk beds. Like Greasewood, we each had a locker for our clothes and personal belongings. I had taken a small bag from home with a few clothes but we were issued clothes by the government and as I remember we all had tops that were the same color, sort of like uniforms. We were each issued a pair of shoes and after I had been there awhile, and partly because of my interest in the Rodeo Club, I was

The bus to Intermountain Indian School.

That's Me (Verna) in the center about to board the Intermountain bus.

Transportation to the bus.

Parents saying goodbye

issued a pair of cowboy boots. Jessie had a pair too, and while they made her taller than shoes, she still stuffed padding in her boots to make her even taller. Intermountain was more than a little bit militarized and we marched in formation everywhere we went, from the dorms to our classes, from class to the dining hall, always in formation. Apparently, some students had figured out that if they got back in formation after their meal, they could get a second meal. But I wouldn't do that, would I? Well...maybe. That was stopped by stamping each student's hand as we entered the dining hall.

Verna and her big sis Jessie.

I liked being at Intermountain and away from my abusive step dad, and being there with my older sister, that I admired, made it special. But like most kids we would pick on one another. We had bunk beds at Intermountain and for a while my sister had the top bunk and I was below. I persisted in bouncing my sister with my feet and legs until the dorm aide stopped it by moving me to a different room.

The school was run by the Bureau of Indian Affairs and was surrounded by a fence. We were not allowed to leave the school grounds without permission. A government truck would patrol the perimeter from time to time, so my friends and I would have to time it right so we could climb the fence without being seen and run down to the Arctic Blast close by.

The Arctic Blast (now called Burgers and Scoops) was a shop that served ice cream as well as burgers and fries or onion rings. My order usually included an orange float. I had money from the job that I held at Intermountain as well as what my mom sent me from time to time. Even though the school would occasionally give us permission to go to the Arctic Blast, we would also climb the chain link fence and head for the Arctic Blast at unauthorized times. It was hard to climb over the chain link fence without getting your pants leg caught on the fence wire!

The Arctic Blast (now Burgers n' Scoops) across the street from the former Intermountain Indian School.

Me (Verna) in 2023 reliving the fun times at the Arctic Blast.

Intermountain Indian School is long gone but the big "I" is still on the side of the mountain.

On one occasion one of the girls was spotted climbing back into the school grounds. We were busted because she had to identify who had gone to the Arctic Blast, and we all were given detention for two weeks.

My favorite class in school was math; Well, after Physical Education (P.E.) that is. Sports was a big part of my experience at Intermountain. Again, I played forward on the basketball team. I was on the school track team and excelled in running events, the sprints and the dashes, a natural I guess with my previous running experience at Ganado Public and Greasewood Boarding School. But this running didn't get me in trouble, I got a ribbon instead of detention. In addition, the school offered baseball, softball, tennis and even had a bowling alley. One of my favorite extra-curricular activities was the Rodeo Club, maybe because my boyfriend at the time was in the rodeo club. Although it seemed to be geared mostly toward boys, I loved being a part of it, maybe because of the boys? All of the horse events, cattle events and bull events were geared toward the boys. The one thing that girls were allowed to participate in was the greased pig contest. It was fun, but no, I was never able to catch the pig. One year I was chosen as a candidate for Rodeo Queen and while I was not crowned Rodeo Queen, I was a close runner-up, which made me feel special and proud.

Sometimes doing the right thing or what seems like the right thing can get you in trouble. There were four special needs girls at Intermountain who would kind of stick together. Maybe because I had been picked on in school because of being lighter skinned, because I was sometimes called "half breed," even in high school, I defended the special needs girls. On this particular day one of the other girls was making fun of the special needs girls, calling them the "lost tribe," and as I and a friend defended the four, the name-calling and bullying escalated and we ended up in a fight. Needless to say, we were sent to the principal's office and reprimanded because of the fight. I was convinced that we did the right thing but maybe in the wrong way.

I don't remember how it all happened but because I did not want to return home for summer vacations for obvious reasons, I was placed with foster parents for the summer vacations. The Mormon Church had been active in promoting foster parents for Indian children in earlier years and

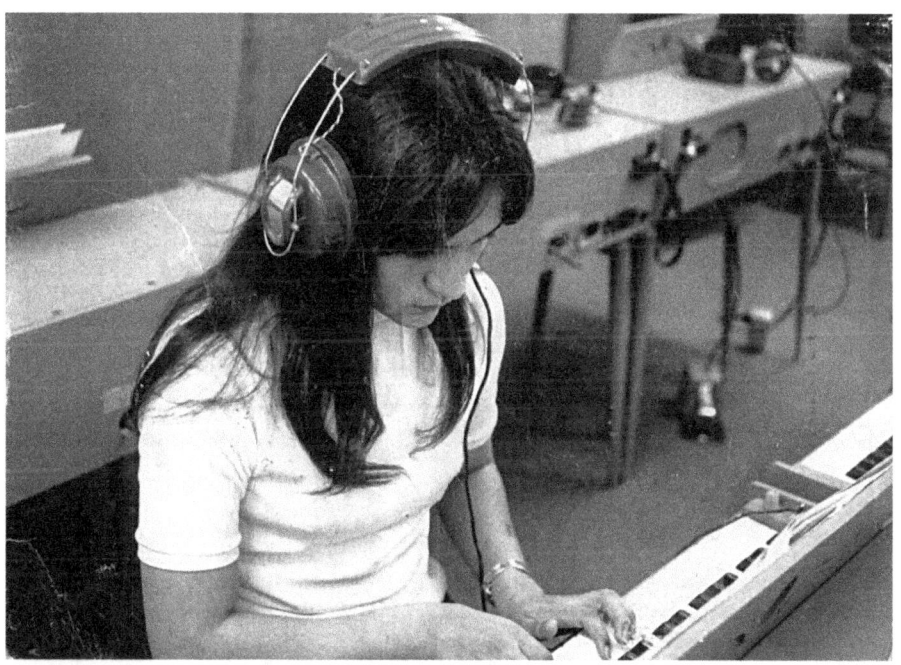

Me (Verna) in piano class at Intermountain Indian School.

```
I dream I...
Was with you
Laughing, talking
Having a good time
Seeing beautiful colors
Around us
Walking hand in hand
Towards the beautiful
Setting sun
Blue, orange, red, purple
Then I woke up...
I was only dreaming.
Only darkness surrounds me
I dream of you every night
If only it weren't dreams
I would be with you
I smile but it's fading
away...
Cause I have lost you
I'll just dream some more.

          Verna Nez
          Freshman
```

Who was I (Verna) dreaming about? I can't remember, but the teacher chose my poem as the best in the class assignment.

Verna's Freshman year at Intermountain Indian School, above.

Project time—That's me (Verna) with the long hair, right.

Future Homemakers of America—That's me (Verna) front center, below.

BOX ELDER JOURNAL, Brigham City, Utah
Thursday, October 14, 1971

New FHA Chapter Organized

OFFICERS — Officers of the New Future Homemakers of America chapter at Intermountain school are pictured, front, from left, Amelia Jean Little, Verna Mae Nez and ? Sam. Second row, Bertha Absley, Mary Tallman and Lillie White.

Newspaper

Me (Verna) at Intermountain Indian School.

Me (Verna) as Rodeo Queen runner-up.

this may have been an offshoot of that program. But whatever it was, it was great for me. My Mormon foster parents were very nice people and I became part of the family. There were three other children besides me in the family and I had a bedroom with one of the daughters. The first summer I remember we went as a family on a vacation in their motor-home and visited among other places what I am sure was Yellowstone National Park with its hot pools and erupting geysers.

I remember watching what was probably Old Faithful and marveling at how it erupted each time right on schedule. The second summer my foster Mom helped me to get a job working at the Dairy Queen, a great experience for someone who had grown up on the Navajo reservation. On Sundays we attended the Mormon Church as we did all through my Intermountain years. I remained at Brigham City for at least three years without going home. I was happy there.

Old Faithful.

Me (Verna) in September 2023 on the steps of what was once Intermountain Indian School where I went to high school.

I'm not quite sure why I went back to Cornfields before I would graduate at Intermountain, but maybe because Jessie had graduated and moved to California and would no longer be there, and besides, I missed my Mom, but maybe just as much on my mind was my latest boyfriend, Richard. Over time my crush on the boy from the Rodeo Club had faded and I was now involved with Richard who would be at home on the reservation, reasonably close to Cornfields. But I wanted to graduate so in the fall I enrolled in the GED program at the College of Ganado, which was located in one of the former Presbyterian Mission buildings.

With my high school diploma in hand, I enrolled in the nurses-aide course at College of Ganado. I didn't know the history at the time, but I have since learned that the mission established by the Presbyterian church at Ganado was, right or wrong, established under the edicts of the Doctrine of Discovery and Manifest Destiny, whereby the church's mission was to convert the Navajos to Christianity and thereby assimilate them into the dominant white culture.

So, as part of the Presbyterian church's mission program, a mission was established and with it a medical clinic in about 1901. By 1903, a day school had been started at the mission, and by 1906, the Ganado Mission Church was completed. Sage Memorial Hospital opened in 1911 and the School of Nursing started in 1930.

As time went on things changed and starting in about the 1960's the public school grew, the government school was closed, and the mission school declined in enrollment and was replaced by the College of Ganado. College of Ganado served me well and I was now qualified for work in a hospital as a nurses-aide.

CHAPTER 5

Na Dene — The People

The Na Dene described in this short chapter were those ancient people who all spoke a similar language and who occupied the northernmost regions of the North American continent. From this group the Diné (Navajo) emerged and migrated to the southwest lands under the direction of Changing Woman to the lands that they currently occupy.

Evidence tends to indicate that my ancestors migrated from the Asian mainland, across the Bering Sea to North America between 10,000 B.C. and 8,000 B.C. They were probably descended from those same people who were led by Genghis Khan as he raided and took possession of territory in formation of the Mongol Empire. Small family groups, hunters in search of game, probably broke off, traveled (walked?) across the ice from Siberia to the North American mainland and with time spread across the northern part of North America in what is now Alaska and Canada all the way to the Hudson Bay. Essentially all of the natives of Canada who speak in the Athapascan style are part of that same group of Asian migrants as the Navajo and the Apache.

As time went on, groups from the north, that would become the Apache and the Navajo, started migrating southward, most of them on the east side of the Rocky Mountains and eventually settled in the area of the four corners (the corners of Utah, Colorado, Arizona and New Mexico) from where they would migrate outward. As my ancestors pushed into the desert that would become their home, they were threatening the inhabitants who were already there, the Tewa and Zuni Pueblo tribes.

It was apparently the Pueblo tribes that named the newcomers the Apache, (*Apachu* which meant strangers or enemies), and it was the Spanish who called those *Apachu* who settled down to farming the *Apaches de las Nabahu* which meant Apaches of the Cultivated Fields. *Apaches de las Nabahu* was later shortened to Navajo even though both the Navajo and the Apache considered themselves *Diné.*

CHAPTER 6

Navajo Tradition and the influence of Changing Woman

The story of "Changing Woman" is the basis for a significant part of the Navajo tradition especially for the women of my tribe, and whether consciously or not, Navajo women attempt to pattern their lives after the example set by Changing Woman. Changing Woman is the model mother. In the Diné creation story, it is Changing Woman's union with the sun, and her sister White Shell Woman's union with the clouds, or water, that give birth to the first Navajo. In that story a turquoise figurine in the shape of a woman becomes the significance of turquoise in Navajo ceremony.

Changing Woman is a goddess of sorts in the tradition of the Diné, both Navajo and Apache. Tradition says that as the *Diné* were preparing to journey to their new home, they wanted Changing Woman to accompany them, but she told them she could not go with them, but she would give them what they needed. She gave them, as told in a publication of the Twin Rocks Trading Post in Bluff, Utah, "food and water to help them grow and prosper, corn for food, corn pollen for offerings, water for ceremonies and to sustain life, dried meat and yucca fruit." It continued to say, "She created the four clans and gave them prayers and songs....She told them to journey to their new homeland within the four sacred mountains where their grandfather, Talking God, awaited them."

These stories become the basis for tradition and ceremony, and the basis for the matrimonial society. A goddess created in the image of the life of the individual and likewise, the life of nature, the life of the earth. Changing Woman would be young as would nature in spring, only to grow old as would nature in fall, and all with the help of the sun and the rain, in everlasting perpetuity. She had not only created the four clans from the flesh of her own body but had given them what they needed.

So, who were the four clans that Changing Woman created? But first, I believe she created clans so that Diné people could know who they were and where they came from. The four original clans were, the *Hashtl'ishnii* —Mud People Clan, the *Kinyaa'áanii* — Towering House Clan, the *Honágháahnii* —One Walks Around You Clan and the *Tódich'ii'nii* — Bitter Water Clan. Currently there are 70 or 80 or more clans. My clan is *Kinłichii'nii* — The Red House People.

And what were the four sacred mountains under whose watchful eye the Diné were directed to establish their homeland. They are the Blanca Peak, which is the highest summit of the Rocky Mountains and is located in present day Colorado, the San Francisco Peaks, the highest point in present day Arizona and located in the north-central part just north of Flagstaff, Mt. Hesperus, the highest point of the La Plata mountains located in present day Colorado and Mt. Taylor, the highest point of the San Mateo mountains located in present day New Mexico northeast of Grants, New Mexico

These stories are the basis of significant tradition, religion and ceremony of the Navajo tribe, and when you look closely, they contain a lot of the same ideas as other religions complete with a unique version of creation and protection of man. One of the most significant ceremonies, in which Changing Woman plays a role, is that ceremony that celebrates the entry into womanhood of a young girl who has just experienced her first or second menstruation. It is a ceremony, a celebration of puberty, where the young girl is the center of attention as the specialness of motherhood is emphasized and the young girl commits herself to that role.

My first experience with this ceremony was when my sister Jessie's menstruation first occurred. My family hurriedly started making plans for the ceremony of puberty in which Jessie would be the center of attention. The ceremony took place at my grandma's hogan. With singing and chanting Jessie was dressed for the occasion after which she was given a softening massage by the women of our family. Her instructions were to run, east to west, twice the first day and three times a day for the next three days, and in between to grind the corn to be used for a huge cake called the *alkaan,* that would be eaten on the ceremony's final day. A pit had been dug in the ground and lined with corn husk in preparation for the batter that she was mixing.

With help, she poured the batter into the husk lined pit and after it was blessed with cornmeal, the batter was covered with corn husks adorned with a cross of husks and then covered with moist dirt. A fire was built on top and kept burning all night to bake the cake. The fourth day was spent in singing after which the cake was uncovered and Jessie was instructed to give a piece to each of the attendees of the ceremony but she was not to eat any herself. One piece was left in the pit as it was covered as a blessing to the earth. This ended the ceremony which had lasted four nights and five days. Jessie was now initiated into womanhood and adulthood. The ceremony, as traditionally celebrated, is designed to follow the example set by Changing Woman.

This is but one of the many ceremonies that make up the traditional Navajo religion. I did not have the honor of having this traditional ceremony performed for me. I was miles away at Intermountain Indian School when I had my first menstruation. When I returned home, my Mom gave me a subdued version of the puberty ceremony, complete with a small corn cake and the traditional running but without the excitement of guests. In a way I felt deprived of having my family involved, but I had chosen to be away at the time the ceremony should have occurred because of intolerable conditions at home.

Navajo women making puberty cake.

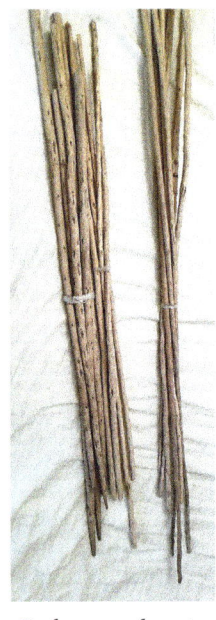

Puberty cake stirring sticks that I (Verna) inherited from my mom.

The Navajo tradition of the puberty ceremony puts a young Navajo girl on the path to adulthood to be brought to reality by the wedding ceremony. I had some boyfriends as I grew up, probably starting with the boy at Greasewood Boarding School who would tease me by pulling my braids, and I would chase him and then we would talk about stuff. At Intermountain Indian School we had a movie theater and a bowling alley that provided opportunities for dates and developing friendships. I had a crush on one of the boys who was in the Rodeo Club. He would take me to a movie and we could hold hands, and maybe steal a kiss, and that was fun. But before long I developed an interest in a boyfriend who had a band that played and sang country songs. Perhaps the reason that my favorite kind of music is Country.

While most of my immediate family no longer lives on the reservation, especially at times of stress we as a family find renewal in both the ceremony and the sweat lodge. A ceremony, complete with the singing of the ceremonial songs, led by a medicine man, and the renewing yucca baths and complete with the rituals of corn meal and corn pollen brings us the continuing blessings of Changing Woman in the Navajo tradition.

The influence of Changing Woman, I believe, is at work in the way my people live their lives, whether intentionally or just because that is the way they were taught. And while modern society is having its influence, the tradition remains.

Tradition says that when the Navajo were preparing to relocate to their new home, Changing Woman gave them what they needed and Changing Woman is considered to have made the first sheep. Sheep are the most important livestock for my tribe and are a symbol of the wealth and vitality of a family. Sheep play a prominent role in many of the traditional ceremonies of the tribe. In past years they provided food for the family, wool for weaving and for clothing and for sale, sheepskins for sale or use and sinew for thread. No wonder the livestock reduction program put in place by the federal government under John Collier was so controversial and so devastating to the Navajo family.

Changing Woman also gave my ancestors corn for food and corn pollen for offerings in preparation for their travel to their new home. The story is that the Sun is corn's father and the Lightning is corn's mother, and when white corn and yellow corn conceived, to them were born two deities one of whom was Talking God, the god who would be waiting for them at their new home. There would be no corn without sun and water. And so, both white corn and yellow corn contribute greatly to the cultural ceremonies.

CHAPTER 7

Marriage and Tradition

Perhaps, no, without question, I grew up in a transition time for my Navajo people. I had spent much of my school years in government boarding schools, schools that had previously used strong-arm tactics in an effort to mold Indian children into the stereotype that the government envisioned; to make them white children. At each of the schools I attended, no longer were students forced to speak only the English language. No longer were students given new names and forbidden to use their Indian names. No longer were Indian children farmed out to white families, for forced labor, during vacation instead of being allowed to go home.

While the Christian churches were a part of the boarding schools I attended, Catholic at Greasewood and Mormon at Brigham City, there was not the pressure to eliminate the Navajo religion. There were no longer missionaries who preached against the Navajo religion as being heathen and who were trying to substitute Christian beliefs like there had been at the Presbyterian mission in Ganado in earlier years before Dr. Salsbury arrived.

Boarding schools had eased up on being quite so militaristic. But still both Greasewood Boarding School and Intermountain Indian School were surrounded by a fence — not to keep predators out but to keep students in, complete with a government vehicle that patrolled from time to time. And still we marched everywhere we went in military style. And still we counted off to make sure no one was missing.

When I finally left Intermountain Indian School and returned to Cornfields, I had not graduated from high school. My boyfriend was Richard. Richard and I had started a relationship back at Intermountain Indian School. He was the lead singer in a country music band which he had organized back during Intermountain days. Richard sang and played guitar. At first, I lived with my Mom in Cornfields and Richard lived close enough that he would pick me up for dates, and we would go to where his band was playing that night. But before long, I moved in with Richard and his parents. That made the temptation too great, we consummated our relationship, and I was pregnant.

Both Richard's parents and my mom were disappointed that we were starting a family so young, but it was what it was. I was very happy being with Richard. Occasionally we talked about the future, but mostly we were just having fun and promoting his band. I was in love and I think Richard was too. We had been a couple for more than three years and I must admit that I dreamed of a life with him.

Richard and I were looking forward to being parents, and he decided to delay returning to Intermountain to finish his schooling. But tragedy was about to strike. I was three or four months into my pregnancy when we loaded the truck with the equipment for that night's performance, but when we arrived at the place the band would be playing that night, we discovered that we had forgotten to load some needed piece of equipment.

So, I took the truck and headed home to retrieve the needed equipment. Part way home, I had a flat tire. What was I to do? I was on a country road with no way to contact anyone. But I knew how to change a tire and that is what I did. That night I lost the baby. We both blamed ourselves but it couldn't be undone.

I still wanted that high school diploma, so as fall term approached I enrolled at the Ganado Public School and rode the school bus back and forth from Cornfields where I was living with my Mom. After about a month I learned that College of Ganado offered a program where you could finish high school and move right on into their nurses-aid training.

My Mom bought a car that I could use for transportation and I transferred to College of Ganado.

Then one day my Mom and stepdad said they wanted to talk to me, and it was then that they told me, my Mom hesitantly, (my Mom knew about Richard; she had met him and knew about our pregnancy) that a certain man wanted to marry me and that I should get married to him. Obviously, I was not part of what had led up to this conversation. I knew about the tradition of the man's family striking a deal with the girl's family whereby the man's family would offer sheep or cattle or jewelry or money or something of value and once the deal was struck they would work together in planning the wedding. But usually the young woman had some say in the choice of a husband.

I really didn't know that much about the man they had chosen to be my husband. Yes, we might had chatted on occasion since he drove the school bus that I rode for a month or so when I attended Ganado Public School to finish my high school education. That must have been when he became enamored with me, when he developed a crush on me, because that is about the only contact we had until our wedding. I could have said no, but they were my parents. I don't remember what I said. But it caught me off guard and maybe I was too surprised to know what to say.

Now, while I really didn't want to, I had to tell Richard that what we had planned could not happen. There were no harsh words. We were heartbroken.

The wedding ceremony took place in my Grandma's hogan. I was dressed in traditional Navajo wedding attire, that my Mom had made for me, in preparation for the ceremony. The guests arrived from both our families and seated themselves, with my husband-to-be's family on one side of the hogan and my family on the other, and the wedding rituals, complete with the sprinkling of corn pollen signifying fertility, were performed by the medicine man in charge, followed by my new husband and I eating corn mush from the wedding basket. After we were given instructions on a successful marriage by the elders and just before the wedding feast began, the wedding blessing was recited;

Now you have lit a fire and that fire should not go out.

The two of you now have a fire that represents love, under-standing and a philosophy of life.

It will give you heat, food, warmth, and happiness.

This new fire represents a new beginning – a new life and a new family.

The fire should keep burning: you should stay together.

You have lit the fire for life, until old age separates you.

Perhaps my new husband wasn't listening. Wasn't there something in the wedding blessing about being faithful to your wife? And where was the fire that the medicine man talked about? And so, I started my married life not based on love but based on tradition.

For a while married life was good and we lived with my new husband's mom. In the beginning she taught me like a daughter: she taught me Navajo skills, weaving rugs, butchering sheep and other skills expected of a Navajo wife. Oh, yes, there were rough spots with my marriage, but my husband had a job, first as a bus driver and later as a maintenance man and he provided for us. He did not drink like so many Navajo men, and he was never abusive to me. And we started a family. And I loved my babies. And I finished my schooling at College of Ganado.

Richard got married and had a family, but eventually turned to drinking. Tragically he was struck by a car and killed while walking on the road. I often wondered whether our breakup had anything to do with his drinking.

Shortly after I finished my training at College of Ganado, we decided to move to Parker, Arizona where my Mom and stepdad were then living. My stepdad's job there was working on transmission line towers. My husband got a job as a heavy equipment operator and after a while I started working at the local school cafeteria. Working in food service at the school caused me to change my hair style from the traditional long hair to having short hair.

I soon became a nurse's aide on the staff of Parker Community Hospital. This was my entry into the health care field and the first use of my nurse's aide training. We only stayed in Parker for a few years but it was an exciting stay not only because I finally got a chance to work in my chosen field of medicine but also because my only son was born while we lived there.

So back to the Navajo Reservation we moved where within a few months I gave birth to my seriously premature youngest and last child with my husband. We had gone to Gallup, New Mexico to do some shopping that day. As we shopped, I started not feeling well and it was getting worse, so we decided to rent a motel for the night so I could lay down until I felt better. But that didn't help, and in the middle of the night I started having severe pains and my water broke.

My husband called the paramedics and off to the Gallup Indian Medical Center I was whisked to not only deal with my serious blood loss with blood transfusions, but to deliver my baby girl. No bigger than the palm of my hand, she spent three months in the pediatric ward in Gallup,

College of Ganado classroom building.

New Mexico, before I finally got to take her home. I stayed with her the whole time until she was allowed to go home. Probably because of my medical training, I was allowed to be somewhat involved with her care in the incubator. That was a scary time but it all worked out and my baby girl is now an adult woman with children of her own.

I had spent months agonizing over the repeated rumors I was hearing about my husband's adultery. I wanted out, but I had seven young children; how could I manage? It was probably the hardest decision of my life, but when I found out that my husband was trying to start an affair with my youngest sister (yes, she told me about it), I'd had enough. With fear and anger in my heart, I filed for divorce. I thought that would end it but when my husband was served with the divorce papers, he refused to sign them.

Years went by and my ex-husband had started a family with another woman and I was in a common law marriage with another man with whom I had two daugh-

My (Verna's) Mom when living in Parker, AZ.

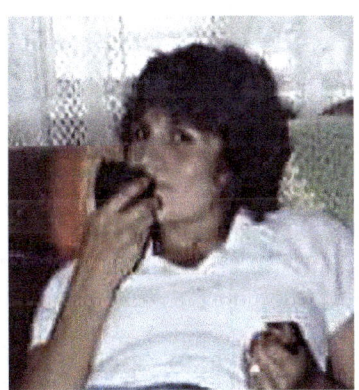

Me (Verna) with short hair.

ters. Finally, after several years, the judge decided that this was absurd and signed the final divorce decree without my husband's signature.

CHAPTER 8

Grandma's Stories of Long, Long Ago

On long winter evenings on the Reservation, Grandma would tell us stories. She told us about how the Spirit People made their way through the first worlds, trying to find a world where they would fit in and flourish. The first world was inhabited by the Insect People. It was a barren world with no plants. They fought among themselves, especially over adultery, but they just couldn't seem to stop committing adultery. They were not welcome there, and they soon found a way to emerge into the second world.

The second world was where the Swallow People lived and like the first world, was a barren world. And again, it was adultery that caused the Spirit People to search for and find a path to the third world.

The third world was the home of the Yellow Grasshopper People, another barren world, and again the Spirit People were asked to leave because of their adultery. They succeeded in finding a path to the fourth world, but as they escaped the third world, four grasshoppers went with them. And that is why to this day we have grasshoppers to contend with.

Grandma did not have electricity in her Hogan, so when the sun went down it was time for stories. And while I recognize bits and pieces of what I remember Grandma telling us when I hear reference to it especially in ceremonies, my memory has dimmed over time and so I am using the book written by Paul G. Zolbrod, *Diné Bahané — The Navajo Creation Story* in writing this chapter. I would highly recommend this book to anyone who wants to read the story in more detail. Zolbrod has translated the poetry, the songs, of the past into text for us to read.

In the fourth world, which was a world inhabited by people who live in upright houses, the Spirit People, sometimes referred to as Insect People, found welcome. They were taken in and fed, and they saw that this world was not barren but that these people had irrigated fields where they were raising food. The Spirit People were happy here and decided to mend their ways, so when the Gods asked them to clean themselves up in preparation for things to come, they did just that.

The next time the Gods visited them, one of the Gods brought two ears of corn, one yellow and one white. They laid out a buckskin on the ground and on top they laid the two ears of corn. Over the two ears of corn, they placed another buckskin. Under the white ear of corn, they placed a white eagle feather and under the yellow ear of corn they placed a yellow eagle feather. The Wind then blew under the buckskin and when the buckskin was removed, there was a man and a woman, First Man and First Woman, the first ancestors of the Navajo people.

They were instructed to live as husband and wife and in four days First Woman gave birth to a set of twins who were both hermaphrodites. After another four days, another set of twins were born which were one male and one female who matured in another four days and lived as husband and wife. In another four days First Woman again gave birth to a set of twins, again one male and one female, and again they matured in four days and lived as husband and wife.

The process continued until five sets of twins having been born with only the first set being hermaphrodites. They then developed a farm and built a dam for irrigation, put the hermaphrodites in charge of guarding the dam and were becoming successful, but the marriages they were in were incestual and that they struggled with. They solved that by just leaving their spouses and marrying other spouses.

Not so fast, thought First Woman. She had to figure out a way for spouses to be more attracted to one another so marriages would be permanent. Her solution was to fashion private parts for the men made of turquoise and private parts for the women made of white and red shell. She now had a plan, she thought, so that couples would be eager to care for each other, share in each other's needs and have children to populate the world. But after that was done, she worried that she had overdone it so she instructed them to keep their private parts covered.

They were being successful in the fourth world and First Man did his part by teaching the people the names of things and the ways of the Gods. He taught them what to do and what not to do and the people gained respect for him and obeyed him.

But then after several years, First Man and First Woman got into an argument. First Woman accused First Man of gathering food for her only so he could get sexual favors, and that angered First Man. He proclaimed to the men of the village: "The women think they can live without us." He led the men to the other side of the river, taking all the things they had invented or made along with them. They also took the hermaphrodites. They took only what they had produced without the help of women, and left everything the women had made for themselves or that they had made together.

For a while, both men and women were happy and would taunt each other from across the river. Within four years, the men had plenty to eat but the women were starving. But both men and women were becoming miserable; they craved sexual satisfaction. So, both men and women turned to masturbation, even though they knew that was not the answer. Finally, First Man and First Woman apologized to each other from across the river and life resumed as it had been before the argument.

Then one day, floods were discovered approaching them from all four directions—they would be drowned unless they could come up with a solution. By the magical powers of the time, a reed was caused to grow that they could enter as it grew to a height that was above the flood water. Once they were above the flood water, First Man and First Woman were able to lead them into the fifth world.

But they were tormented until they discovered that the Coyote had accompanied them. He had stolen two infants from the fourth world and the floods of the fourth world were angry. Once the infants were thrown back into the hole through which they had escaped into the fifth world, the anger stopped.

Not long after that, one of the hermaphrodites stopped breathing, so its body was laid to rest among the rocks. But when they returned to view the body, it was gone. They searched everywhere but could not find it. Then two men peered into the hole through which they had emerged into the fifth world, and there they saw the hermaphrodite sitting by a river combing her hair. Four days later, those same two men died. That is the reason the Navajo people refuse to look at a dead body or stare at a ghost.

It seems that the Pueblos had built a camp close by where they were and it became known that the Pueblos had brought an ear of corn with them from the fourth world. They argued about who should have the ear of corn, and some of the more reasonable ones decided they should break the ear in half so they could share. While they were trying to decide which group should get which half, the coyote made off with the tip end, so the Pueblo assumed the Navajo had made their choice. This is why the Pueblo always grow better corn than the Navajo. This whole incident caused hard feelings and is why the Pueblo and the Navajo live far apart.

First Man and First Woman then decided to make their world better. They built seven sacred mountains with four on the edges and three in the middle. The four on the edges were Sierra Blanca Peak on the east, Mount Taylor on the south, San Francisco Peak on the west and Big Mountain Sheep on the north. These four mountains they placed where the water flowing from the fourth world gathered after it seeped through the holes. The three mountains in the middle were Travelers Circle, Giant Spruce and Butte Piled on a Butte. They then set about creating the land with its animals and birds.

The world was dark, so they made the sun and the moon to light the land. Then, they needed to give it life so it could serve the Earth Surface People that would eventually be created. At night it was still too dark, so they created stars. They had a plan to place the stars in an orderly pattern, but the coyote thought they were too slow and hurled the stars into the haphazard positions we see today.

During their travels in the fifth world, they often encountered women who were pleasuring themselves with various objects. This would result in the births of monsters, and this is how the fearful monsters came to be.

By relocating to the west, they had a decade or more of rather blissful living where the people and the animals lived together as equals. But then the monsters showed up and started killing them and eating their bodies. They moved again, but then the monsters found them.

They then found refuge at a great pueblo at Chaco Canyon that was built by the Pueblos already living there. It had not been built willingly. As the story goes, a Gambling God showed up and challenged the Pueblos to games of chance, and before long the Gambling God owned all their property, their women and children and even some of their men. The Gambling God made a bargain with the remaining Pueblos that if they would build him a great village, he would return their property, as well as the women, children and men he owned.

The Pueblos got busy building, which is about the time that the wanderers trying to escape the monsters showed up. Other villages heard about the Gambling God and came to try their luck, but the Gambling God always won. Thus, his village was built rapidly by the slaves he won. The Air-spirit people from whom the Navajos are descended remained onlookers while this went on.

Then Talking God appeared and announced there would be a ceremony because the Sun was unhappy with the Gambling God. With plans completed, the followers of Talking God were able to outwit the Gambling God and win everything back. Eventually they shot the Gambling God into the air like an arrow and he landed at the dwelling of the God, Grabber of Women's Breasts. The Breast Grabber took pity on the Gambling God and made new wealth for him, but when he sent him back, he made him God to a new people. He made him God to the Mexicans and sent him to what is now Old Mexico.

The Spirit People learned from this to never behave contrary to the Gods and to never despise the poor and the humble, because those you despise may be favored by the Gods.

Soon after the Gambling God had been shot into the air, those that would become Navajos left that place and entered a period of distrust. The antics of the coyote resulted in death and despair.

There was a young woman and twelve brothers who lived together at this place. At first the twelve brothers had made friends with the coyote because the coyote was a good hunter and could round up game and herd it toward the brothers so it was easy for them to kill the game for food.

The coyote wanted to marry the beautiful maiden who was their sister, but the sister said she would not marry him. Finally, she told him that she would not marry anyone unless they had killed at least one of the monsters that pursued them. The coyote succeeded in doing just that, and finally he married the beautiful maiden. After he had consummated the marriage, he urinated all around the maiden's lodge to mark his territory.

When the maiden's brothers returned, the stench of the coyote was everywhere. The coyote and the maiden were forced to leave the home of the brothers. The brothers didn't trust the coyote and assigned one brother to act as a lookout.

On one of their hunting trips, the brothers concocted a plan that got the coyote killed. When the hunting party returned home, the maiden asked where her husband was and the brothers told her to forget him.

Using the magic she had gotten from her husband the coyote, she was able to eventually kill all the brothers except the youngest one by changing herself into a she-bear. Eventually the youngest brother killed his sister, the she-bear. After looking at her corpse, he cut off her nipples and threw them into the pinyon tree. Up until then the pinyon tree had been barren of fruit, but from that time on pinyon trees produced edible pine nuts.

With the help of the Holy Ones the twelve brothers were brought back to life, but from that time on they never trusted the coyote who had caused so much disorder in their lives.

These people who would become the Navajo now called themselves the Emergence People, and they were still trying to escape the monsters. They continued to settle in a place and grow crops only to be discovered by the monsters who would kill and devour them. Finally, only six remained: First Man and First Woman, one elderly man and wife and two children, one a young man and one a young woman.

They were about ready to give up trying to get away from the monsters. They didn't know which Gods were their friends and which Gods were their enemies. Then, First Man saw a dark cloud descending on Giant Spruce Mountain. He wanted to go investigate but First Woman was afraid for his life. He went anyway, singing as he went in hopes that his singing would protect him from danger.

As he reached the peak, with lightning flashing around him, he heard a cry like an infant. It was dark and raining heavily, but he made his way to the spot of the crying, and as he reached the spot the storm stopped. He looked down, and there at the spot where he had heard the infant crying he saw a turquoise figure. The figure was in the shape of a female and was about the size of a newborn baby. First Man picked the turquoise figure up and carried it back to First Woman.

Two days later, Talking God appeared to them and gave them instructions to bring the other four survivors and go to the top of Giant Spruce Mountain in twelve nights. They did as they were instructed and Talking God and Growling God met them there. They looked around and saw all of the prominent people they had encountered in the previous worlds.

White Body stood there holding a figurine very much like the one First Man and First Woman carried, except it was fashioned of white shell instead of turquoise. They were instructed to hand both figurines to the Mirage Stone People.

Talking God then laid a buckskin on the ground with its head facing west. The Mirage Stone People laid the two figurines on the buckskin with their heads pointing west. They also laid two ears of corn on the buckskin, one white ear and one yellow ear, with their points to the west. Talking

God placed another buckskin on top facing east. The attendees formed a circle, leaving a space for the Wind to approach, and the ceremony began.

The two Gods, Talking God and Growling God, raised a corner of the buckskin slightly three different times and the Wind blew his magic. The fourth time the two Gods raised the top buckskin, they saw that both ears of corn and the two figurines were now living people.

The turquoise figurine was now Changing Woman, the White Shell figurine was now White Shell Woman, the white ear of corn was now White Corn Boy and the yellow ear of corn was now Yellow Corn Girl.

Quoting from the book *Diné Bahane' The Navajo Creation Story*, page 179, "It was the wind who gave them life; the very wind that comes from four directions. The very wind that comes out of our own mouths now as we speak and breathe. The wind that brings spirit into our bodies from everywhere and which, when it ceases to blow inside of us, can make us all speechless so that we die, it is said."

Everybody left and White Corn Boy and Yellow Corn Girl were taken to the summit of the mountain where they could reside with the Gods.

Soon Changing Woman and White Shell Woman became lonely and decided to present themselves, Changing Woman to the Sun, and White Shell Woman to the water, and both soon found that they were pregnant.

Four days later both women were in labor. Talking God gave Changing Woman one end of a strand of sunbeam and asked her to pull with each spasm of labor. Rain God did the same for White Shell Woman. "Which is how it came to pass that Navajo women who walk the surface of this world to this day pull upon a drag rope whenever they deliver new life." (*Diné Bahane' — The Navajo Creation Story,* page 183). Changing Woman and White Shell Woman had each birthed a son.

As the young boy's grew, they disobeyed their mothers and hunted far from home. By so doing, they alerted the monsters to their whereabouts. And sure enough, the monsters showed up intent on killing and eating the boys. When the Giant Monster approached their dwelling, the mothers hid their sons. The sons could hear what was going on and they were ashamed that they had disobeyed their mothers and thereby alerted the monsters.

So, they slipped out early in the morning and traveled far, eventually coming to the under- ground dwelling of Spider Woman. She offered them help if they would tell her who they were and what their mission was. Finally, they told her what they had done and that they were fleeing from the monsters. But they said, "We don't know who we are, we don't know who our father is. We are fleeing in disgrace."

Spider Woman welcomed them and said she would tell them who their father was — and about his dwelling and how to get there. She also told them she would tell them how they could seek his help. She fed them and then told them that their father was the Sun, but the path there was dangerous and had risk of monsters.

"There are four places," she said, "that men cannot survive," and she gave them a talisman that would protect them. She then taught them the song they were to sing in the face of danger. She placed the sacred talisman in a medicine bundle and sent them on their way.

When they came to the Rocks that Crush, they did as they were told by Spider Woman and they passed through safely. Next came the Slashing Reeds with leaves as sharp as knives. They worked with the monsters and using the instruments the Spider Woman had provided they were allowed to pass unharmed.

Next, they came to the Giant Awl Cactus area. These cacti would jump and pierce trespassers with poisonous thorns. They were part of the monster gang. Again, Spider Woman's instructions worked. Next, they came to the Boiling Dunes, dunes that could burn you to a crisp. Again, the Spider Woman's instructions allowed them to pass.

After making it through several more danger areas, they finally came to the house of their father, the Sun. The entrance was guarded by two bears, but again the Spider Woman's instructions worked. The Sun's house was made of turquoise and was square like a Pueblo house.

At the end of the day, when the Sun came home, he denied that these were his sons. The Sun had a sweat lodge prepared and the twins were ordered to enter. The Sun had intended to get rid of the twins, but the Wind helped them and they survived the heat. Since they survived the sweat lodge, he decided they might be his sons. But he was still not convinced, even as they passed test after test.

Finally, he was convinced and he asked why they had come. They told him that the monsters were destroying them all and wanted help. The Sun said the monsters might also be his sons, but regardless, I will help you by giving you weapons against the monsters. But, he said, I must strike the first blow against the Big Giant. He then gave the twins the weapons they would need. But the Sun had one more test for the twins. Again, the Wind gave them safe passage and finally the Sun believed and made a way for the twins to return home,

When they got home, they were welcomed by a group who knew about the origin of the monsters. How they were birthed by women who used objects to give themselves sexual pleasure and as a result became pregnant and gave birth to monsters including the Big Giant.

The next morning the twins made their way to the Warm Springs. As they waited there, the Big Giant approached. With the help of the weapons the Sun had provided and help from the Wind, Big Giant was killed. They removed Big Giant's scalp as a trophy and then decided to give each other names. One of the twins was thereafter called "He Who Cuts the Life Out of the Enemy" and the other was called "Monster Slayer."

The sons went to visit their mother and told her that they had visited their father, the Sun, and that they had destroyed the Big Giant. At first their mother did not believe them, but they showed her the Big Giant's scalp and she believed and celebrated.

They wanted to kill more monsters, and Monster Slayer convinced his brother that he should go alone to slay the Horned Monster. With the help of the gopher, the ground squirrel and the weapons provided by his father, the Sun, the Horned Monster was killed.

Next, he wanted to go after the Bird Monster, four of them there were, and finally his mother, Changing Woman, told him where they lived. As he climbed the mountains, he came upon two giant snakes who were sunning themselves. He gently walked from one to the other without disturbing them and arrived at the plains. Those snakes turned to stone and are still a bridge between the peaks of the White Spruce Mountains.

As he walked across the plains, a giant creature in the shape of an eagle swooped down at him. Only by lying flat on the ground did he escape its sharp talons. After several tries, the Eagle Monster was successful in getting his talons into Monster Slayer. He then carried him to a high ledge. The Eagle Monster dropped Monster Slayer from high in the sky, expecting him to be killed by the fall so his offspring could feed. But, using the sacred feathers that Spider Woman had given him, Monster Slayer landed gently.

The fledglings prepared to feast on Monster Slayer but were frightened off when he yelled at them. Monster Slayer ordered them to tell him where their father perched when he came back, when he would come back, and also where their mother perched. The fledglings told him all that he asked.

So, he was prepared when the male Eagle Monster returned and fired one of the weapons the Sun had given him at the Eagle Monster. He killed the male Eagle Monster. Then, the female Eagle Monster returned and dropped a finely dressed Pueblo woman on the ledge. When she glided down to another ledge, Monster Slayer used another of the weapons the Sun had given him and he killed the female Eagle Monster as well.

The fledglings feared for their lives, but Monster Slayer used the powers he possessed and changed one of them into the eagles we see today. The other was changed into the owls we see today.

Monster Slayer convinced Bat Woman to help him get down off the ledge and she reluctantly did, but told him he was to keep his eyes closed so he couldn't see how ugly she was. Reluctantly he did so and when he was safely down, he gave her feathers off the dead Eagle Monster to make herself beautiful. He also gave her strict instructions on where not to walk, but she paid no attention to his instructions and as a result the feathers Monster Slayer had given her magically turned into birds and few away. So, Bat Woman remained ugly, and still is to this day.

Back at the home of his mother and brother, Monster Slayer now wanted to know where Kicking Monster lived. Reluctantly his mother told him that Kicking Monster lived at Rock Ridge. So, early the next morning,

Monster Slayer went off to find Kicking Monster. He was the monster who waited by the rocks where travelers would warm themselves in the sun and then would kick them over the cliff to their deaths.

As Kicking Monster tried to kick Monster Slayer off the cliff, Monster Slayer was able to kill him with the knife provided by his father, the Sun. As Kicking Monsters' body fell into the valley below, Monster Slayer could hear Kicking Monster's children quarreling over the tasty morsels of their father's body.

When Monster Slayer got to the valley floor, he found twelve Kicking Monster children. All but one he was able to kill with the knife given to him by his father, the Sun. When Monster Slayer caught that last one who had run away, he was about to kill him but he was so ugly that he decided to banish him to a life of living off dead bodies. He was transformed into a buzzard and remains as a buzzard today.

When Monster Slayer returned home, he asked his mother, Changing Woman, the whereabouts of the Monster That Kills with His Eyes. Again, reluctantly she told him that monster lived at Black Hole Rock, so Monster Slayer left for that place. He took with him a bag of salt and the weapons given him by his father, the Sun.

When Monster Slayer entered the home of the Monster That Kills with His Eyes, he sat by the wall. The monster couple with many children glared at Monster Slayer, but his armor protected him. Monster Slayer then threw salt into the fire, which hissed, sputtered and threw sparks that landed on the monsters' eyes and blinded them.

With the monsters blind, Monster Slayer could easily kill all but two of the youngest fearful staring kids. Monster Slayer told these two that he was going to let them live, but he was going to change their destinies. One he changed into an Exploring Bird whose mission was to warn the five-fingered Earth Surface People of approaching danger. The other one he changed into a whippoorwill whose mission was to sing beautifully to make the world a happy place.

When Monster Slayer returned home, his mother, Changing Woman, sang a song of rejoicing. But Monster Slayer was not done. Now he asked for the whereabouts of Tracking Bear Monster. Again, reluctantly his mother told him that the Tracking Bear Monster lived at Reticence Rock.

So, the next morning Monster Slayer left for Reticence Rock. When he approached Reticence Rock, he saw that the Tracking Bear Monster's den was in the shape of a cross with entrances facing in all four directions. When the Tracking Bear Monster stuck his head out of his den, Monster Slayer cut off his head with the knife given him by his father, the Sun. Monster Slayer picked up the head and spoke to it, saying from this day forward its mission was to do good rather than evil.

He cut the head in three pieces with the knife given him by his father, the Sun. One piece he threw east to become the yucca fruit plant with a mission of nourishing the people of the future. The second piece he threw west to become the yucca soapsuds plant that people would use to cleanse themselves. The third piece he threw south to become the mescal fiber plant that people could use to make thread.

So, Monster Slayer went home to rest for four days. Then he would kill more monsters.

There was White Monster Under the Rock, and Yellow Monster Under the Rock and Black Giant Under the Rock and Brown Giant Hiding in the Earth, as well as various animals that lived among the Pueblo ruins that still needed to be gotten rid of to make the land safe.

The two brothers talked about how they could finish the job and decided that they should visit their father, the Sun, again. After some verbal maneuvering, the sons and the Sun came to an agreement. The Sun would help rid the world of the remaining monsters and the sons would help convince their mother, Changing Woman, to establish a home in the west where Changing Woman and the Sun could live together.

On their way home, Monster Slayer and his brother, Child of Water, had a vision. They saw a country of five-fingered Earth Surface People who would someday be known as Navajo, once the monsters were disposed of. With joy in their hearts, they sang as they walked.

But when they attempted to give the things to Changing Woman that the Sun asked them to give to her, the hoops, the knives and hailstones, she refused them saying she cared nothing about them. As she talked, it became evident that she was upset that the Sun had paid no attention to her. As they continued to talk, she began to weep and she reached out and accepted the hoops, the hailstones and the knives.

Changing Woman obviously knew what to do with the hoops, the knives and the hailstones, and after she had done that and the weather had reacted in response, she walked away alone to the lodge where she had given birth to her offspring.

For four days, the world was so dark that neither the sun nor the moon was seen. On the fifth day, the sky cleared and there were four days of good weather. Then, the sky grew dark again and a thick white cloud descended.

For days, the violent storm continued. They were fearful for their home, and Monster Slayer devised a way to secure it. The storm was so violent that not even a monster could survive such wind and such hail.

When the storm was over, much good change had occurred to the world and Changing Woman was sure the monsters had been destroyed. But the Wind whispered to Monster Slayer that the Old Age Woman had survived. Monster Slayer asked his mother, Changing Woman, where he might find Old Age Woman. Changing Woman refused to tell him, but the Wind whispered that Old Age Woman lived at the Place of Mountain Sheep.

So, Monster Slayer was off to find Old Age Woman. When he found One Who Brings Old Age and told her he had come there to kill her, she reasoned with him. She told him that she was the one who saw to it that people eventually got old and died to make room for the younger people. "If you kill me, and that stops happening," she said, "and there will be no incentive for boys to become fathers and girls to become mothers because everyone will live forever. Let me live, and I will inspire people to bring children into the world." Monster Slayer agreed and returned to the home of Changing Woman.

Soon the Wind whispered to him that Cold Woman still lived. "Each year," he said, "she freezes the earth and covers the streams with ice and she kills the plants." Again, Changing Woman would not tell him where Cold

Woman lived, but the Wind whispered that she lived high on the summit where the mountain sheep are, on the north slope just below the peak where the snow never melts.

And so, the next day Monster Slayer was off to find her. When he found her naked and shivering, he told her that he was there to kill her so that the earth people would not have to suffer each year. "I am miserable here," she said, "and don't care if you kill me. But, you need to know what the consequences of my death would be. Once I am dead, it will always be hot on the earth. The land will eventually dry up from not having a season of rest. The springs will stop flowing once all the snow melts, and eventually all plants and even the people will die." After hearing that, Monster Slayer turned around and went home.

Again, the Wind whispered in his ear that Poverty Creatures still live and they will destroy people by using up their possessions, leaving no tools and no clothes to wear. Again, Changing Woman refused to give him directions, but the Wind told him these creatures live at Roof Butte Mountain.

Off Monster Slayer went to find them. What he found was a tattered old man and a filthy old woman who had nothing. When Monster Slayer told them he had come to kill them, they replied that he should stop and think what that would mean. "If we die," they said, "people would wear the same clothes day after day and year after year. There would be no reason to replace anything. But if we continue to wear things out, people will use their ingenuity to make things stronger and more beautiful and designs of all kinds will improve." Monster Slayer turned around and went home.

Again, Monster Slayer set out, this time to find Hunger Man who lived at White Spot of Grass. But he was soon convinced that were hunger gone, people would lose their taste for food, would not have the pleasure of cooking and eating and would have no reason to grow crops or raise livestock or go hunting. Again, Monster Slayer turned around and went home.

Monster Slayer now realized that his job was done and he shed the weapons his father, the Sun, had given him.

Monster Slayer made a trek across the land and found nothing but peace and friendship. As he sang a song of rejoicing, he heard another song coming from the east. It was his father, the Sun, who seemed to be pleased. He arranged to have all the monsters' bodies buried in one spot. He then took the trophies Monster Slayer had collected and the weapons he had loaned to Monster Slayer, saying, "If you need them again, they are here."

As he left, he said he would return in four days, this time with a message for Changing Woman. He then asked Monster Slayer to tell her to meet him at the summit of Giant Spruce Mountain.

On the morning of the fifth day, Changing Woman made her way to the summit of Giant Spruce Mountain. As she rested on a rock, she recognized the place as the place where she had first offered herself to the Sun.

The Sun wanted her to come to the west and make a home for him. They bargained for some time but finally decided they would provide to each other the things that the other wanted. With that agreement, Changing Woman agreed to live with the Sun in the west. She bid farewell to her sister, White Shell Woman, and her sons Monster Slayer and Water Born, and departed for her new home in the west. She left with Gods and animals to accompany her to her retirement home.

When they came to San Francisco Mountain, they laid Changing Woman across the very top of the mountain, with her head to the west. They massaged her body and stretched her limbs. This ceremony became the ceremony performed on all young Navajo girls on their way to womanhood.

Changing Woman arrived at her floating house beyond the shore where the Sun joins her still to this day at the end of each day.

When Changing Woman went to live with the Sun in the west, White Shell Woman headed for the San Juan Mountain. Monster Slayer and Water Born went with White Shell Woman as far as the Place Where Two Waters Join in the valley of the San Juan River.

White Shell Woman thought she would be happy living in the mountains surrounding the Emergence Place, but she soon became lonely. As she awoke one morning, she was visited by Talking God. He asked her how she had survived not being eaten by the monsters. She told him where she had been with her sister and that she thought she would be happy in the mountains but now she was lonely. He told her to stay where she was for four days and then he would visit again and bring Changing Woman and others with him.

On the fifth day, the Talking God returned and with him was Growling God and others that she couldn't make out in the darkness. The people who were there arranged themselves in four groups: East, West, South and North. In the East were Holy People from Sierra Blanca Peak, in the South from Blue Bead Mountain, in the West from Water Cloud Mountain and in the North from Mountain Sheep Mountain.

White Shell Woman went among the West group but was told by Changing Woman that the West was her group, so White Shell Woman should go to the East group.

Changing Woman had brought two sacred blankets with her, one had dark embroidery and one had white embroidery. Talking God had brought two sacred buckskins and the Divine Couple had brought two ears of corn, one white and one yellow that they carried in a turquoise dish.

Talking God laid the sacred blankets carefully on the ground and on them he spread one of the sacred buckskins with the head to the west. From the turquoise dish Talking God took the white ear of corn and handed it to Rock Crystal Boy of the Eastern Mountain, and the yellow ear he handed to Yellow Corn Girl of the Western Mountain. These Holy People laid the ears of corn on the buckskin with the tip of the yellow ear pointing west and the tip of the white ear pointing east. They backed away and Talking God picked up the ears and placed them against the buckskin with tips pointing east, but he did not actually let them touch anything.

He held them there and uttered his cry. Then he nearly laid them down but scarcely touched the buckskin. He then uttered the cry of Growling God. He repeated that, pointing the ears in each of the four directions. So, the two ears of corn were made to face each of the four cardinal directions. And so it is that Navajo people never dwell in villages like Pueblo people, but live in small houses scattered across the land.

Over the ears of corn, the Talking God laid the other sacred buckskin with the head facing east. The Wind entered between the skins. When he finally lifted a corner of the top buckskin, the white ear of corn had become a man and the yellow ear of corn had become a woman. These were the five-fingered Earth Surface People. The Wind had created this life just like he still does to this day.

Once the Wind had given them life, the Rock Crystal Boy of the Eastern Mountain gave them each a mind and the Yellow Corn Girl of the Western Mountain gave them each a voice. When the top buckskin was completely removed, a dark cloud descended and covered the bodies of the pair like a blanket.

White Shell Woman led the new couple into her Hogan and everyone else left. Before he left, Talking God promised to return in four days.

This was the beginning of the Navajo Nation.

Four days later when Talking God returned, he brought with him another couple, Sky Mirage Boy and Ground Mist Girl. When he got there, he gave White Shell Woman two ears of corn and instructed her to grind them one grain at a time.

White Shell Woman explained to the couple that had just arrived that the couple there with her had also been made from corn and they cannot marry because they are brother and sister. She suggested that maybe they could marry the couple that had been made from corn so that children could be brought into the world. And that is how the first married couples came to be.

The young man made from white corn married Ground Mist Girl and the young girl made from yellow corn married Mirage Boy. From these people the clan known as Honeycombed Rock People was formed.

This clan did not know that any others existed, but with the help of the Wind they found the clan Place Where the Channel Narrows, who were having a hard time finding game and plants to eat. The Honeycombed Rock clan invited the Place Where the Channel Narrows clan to join them. Perhaps their condition was a little better. This is the group that is known as the Rock Corner People today.

On the morning that the two clans got together, Talking God again came to visit White Shell Woman. They talked secretly. Three days later, Talking God again visited and again they talked secretly.

White Shell Woman told the young girl who had become her favorite that she would be going away, because she was no longer needed there. No one knew where she had gone, but in a dream she told the young girl that she had gone to live with the Gods and would live in the house of white shell forever. She would not be with them in the form they knew her in, but she would still be with them in the form of the gentle rain.

The new group moved in search of more game and eventually found a suitable place and learned how to plant the corn that had been given to White Shell Woman by Talking God. They found that it produced much with the help of gentle rain. Fourteen years later, a group called Travelers Circle clan joined them and they lived together. After seven more years, another clan arrived called the Yucca Strung Out in a Line clan.

After fourteen more years, the growing Navajo tribe moved on to the Broad House Place in the Chaco Canyon where they occupied the ruins there and built campfires. The campfires attracted strangers from a distant mountain. They were the Gray Streak clan and they joined the tribe too.

There were now five groups in the Navajo nation and they moved to the banks of the San Juan River. They settled at a place called Tree Sweeping Water, because of the trees by the stream. They decided this is where they would stay. After six years in this place, another band joined them called the Dark Streak of Wood clan. They had with them a wise man, a chief called Something Inspired Him to Lecture.

They prospered in the San Juan River Valley, but life was hard. They lived on game they could catch and plants they could grow. They did not yet have horses or sheep or goats or any domestic animals. They had hides to make clothing from the game they killed, and they learned to weave clothing from cedar bark.

As their population grew, the valley where they lived became crowded and they started spreading to other areas. Eight years after the Dark Streak of Wood clan joined the tribe, another clan, the Tangle People, joined the tribe. They were descendants of the Mirage People.

After five more years, another group called the Mountain Cove clan joined the tribe. They were similar to the Tangle People, so those two clans grew very close, so close that now the members of the one clan cannot marry into the other. This clan brought with them the skill of making wicker water bottles and carrying baskets, as well as how to make earthen pots.

Five years later, another group joined the tribe. They had come from White Shore, which was located near what is now Santa Fe. After a while, they were formed into the Water's Edge clan. They settled at what would be called Trail Leading Upward, where they found soil suitable for growing crops. They also had a chief called Big Knee who taught them to put stakes where they intended to plant. They were skilled hunters and had many buckskins they made into beautiful shirts and coats. They taught the other clans this skill.

The two chiefs worked together to perfect the language because they did not all speak the same and this would help them communicate.

The Water's Edge clan remained at the Trail Leading Upward for thirteen years. During that time, Chief Big Knee had taken twelve wives, four from the Dark Streak of Wood clan, four from the Mountain Cove clan and four from the Tangle clan. He traded large amounts of grain for these wives, but that did not win their affection and they were unfaithful to him.

The chief complained to the three clans and although they did not like the chief, they also disliked adultery. The clans asked the wives to be faithful, but they continued to be unfaithful. The tribesmen suggested that the chief had done nothing to gain the affection of his wives, but still they gave him permission to punish his unfaithful wives.

So, Big Knee cut out the genitals of the next wife who was unfaithful and she died. When another wife was unfaithful, he cut off her ears and she also died. When the third wife was unfaithful, he cut off her breasts and she, too, died. When a fourth committed adultery, he cut off her nose. While she did not die, she was marked for life as a woman guilty of adultery.

So, Big Knee and the other men decided cutting off the nose would be the punishment for adultery. This didn't work, and soon all of his wives were without a nose and they made no secret of their hatred for him. No one would sleep with him, so he was alone.

Even though he deserved it, the people felt sorry for Chief Big Knee and they held a ceremony for him. This was to be a nine-night ceremony and for eight nights the remaining wives stayed in a hut by themselves and talked about Big Knee's cruelty and about how easily the other men gave in to him. They decided to leave; they were not slaves.

On the ninth night of the ceremony called the Mountain Chant, everyone was expected to join in the circle of dancing. When the nine surviving wives appeared, they each carried a sharp knife. As they danced, Big Knee became afraid and hid himself. The wives danced and sang, brandishing the knives. They were chanting, "The knife has disfigured me."

No man had the courage to get close to them. Soon, the wives were the only ones still in the circle dancing. As they danced, they left the place and went far to the north. That is where they still live today. From time to time, they resume their curse on the Navajo people. When they start their angry cries, the north wind blows, bringing snow and strong winds in the winter and heavy rain and lightning in the summer.

Soon after the nine-day ceremony for Chief Big Knee, a group of Utes visited the Navajo. They stayed for a full season and helped with the crops, leaving in the fall with grain to help get them through the coming winter. But one family remained, an older couple with two daughters and one son. While they always intended to leave, they ended up staying until they died.

They had become especially good friends with the Water's Edge clan and eventually married into that clan, and the Sage Brush Hill People resulted. So, the Water's Edge clan and the Sage Brush Hill People are so closely related that they are not allowed to marry within these clans.

Soon after the Utes left, the Navajo were visited by another band and because of their similarity they joined the Water's Edge clan.

Sometime later, a group of Apache broke off and wanted to become Navajo. They called themselves Black Rock Standing Like a Wall clan. They, too, associated so closely with the Water's Edge clan that they may not marry within that clan.

About the same time, a famine hit the Zuni pueblo and some starving Zuni came to join the Navajo. Another group joining the tribe was given the name, Clan from the Place Near the Water. Other groups, Red Extends into the Water as well as the Willow People, also joined the Navajo tribe. Where the Navajo once had been small and weak, they had now become numerous and strong.

Certain clans seemed to have not been bothered by the monsters. Some thought the great pueblos might know why. So, a restless young warrior led a party to raid the pueblo called *Kinłichii'nii* which means Red House. Days later, they returned with several captives. Among them was a young girl that the warrior himself had captured. She became his wife and the mother of his many children, and eventually died a respected Navajo woman.

From her came the clan *Kinłichii'nii* meaning Red House clan. This is the clan *Kinłichii'nii*, Red House clan to which I belong. This clan is closely related to the Black Horizontal Forest People, which is the clan of the warrior who led the raid. So, these are two clans that must not marry.

At first the captives were treated as slaves but they participated fully with the Navajo and soon became free. From these captives, another clan, the Many Goats clan, emerged. It is also closely related to the Black Horizontal Forest People.

A band of Apaches from the south joined the tribe as two clans, Start of the Red Streak People and Red Bottom People. Then, another group of Utes arrived and became Ute People clan.

Soon the Ute People assembled a war party and raided a Mexican settlement at what is now Socorro. They captured a Spanish woman who was first made a slave but then married one of the young men. She, too, bore many children and died a respected Navajo woman. Their clan is People Who Move About or they are sometimes called the Mexican clan. These members cannot marry into the Ute clan.

While young warriors were busy raiding Spanish settlements, Chief Big Knee, who was now old and feeble, was trying to restore his health and good fortune. He was hoping that a ceremony called *Naachid* could reverse his aging. Some strangers had heard of the ceremony and came to attend.

They were eventually adopted into the tribe as the Where the Waters Join clan.

Another group of Apaches visited to witness the ceremony of Chief Big Knee and stayed overnight. When they left, one of the Navajo girls went with them and the resulting marriage between her and an Apache man resulted in the Yellow People clan.

Changing Woman was now living in the west with her husband, the Sun. With her husband gone all day, she was becoming lonely. *Perhaps the Earth Surface People might keep me company,* she thought, *like they did for my sister, White Shell Woman.* So, from the skin of her left arm she created two full grown males and two adult females. From these two couples, a clan would be formed. Eventually they would become the He Walks Around One clan, but not yet.

Next, from the skin of her right arm, she created four Earth Surface People—two adult males and two adult females. From these two couples, another clan would descend. Eventually that clan would become the Towering House People, but not yet.

Next, from skin under her left breast, she created two adult males and two adult females. From these four would descend another clan, which would eventually be the Bitter Water clan, but not yet. In like fashion, from the skin under her right breast she created two adult men and two adult women. From these couples another clan would be formed and would eventually be the Within His Cover People clan, but not yet.

Then from the skin midway between her two breasts, she created two adult males and two adult females. This clan would eventually be called Mud clan, but not yet. Lastly, from a spot of skin on her back, midway between her shoulder blades, she created two adult men and two adult women. Eventually this clan would be called Close to Her Body clan, but not just yet.

She told these twelve couples that they were created to dwell near her and be her companions. She took them from her floating home to the mainland, and they lived there for thirty years and multiplied. At the end of the thirty years, the twelve couples that remained called their offspring, the People of the Twelve, together and told them about the sister's people in the east and that they might want to go there.

But first they made a visit to their mother, Changing Woman, which was accomplished via a rainbow bridge from the mainland to the floating house. Changing Woman embraced each of the surviving ten and then she replaced the two that had died by fashioning them out of sacred turquoise. So, after being invited to do so, the twelve decided to stay with Changing Woman and their offspring decided to join the offspring of White Shell Woman in the east.

Since it would be a dangerous journey to the east, Changing Woman gave them five of her pets: the Gentle Deer, the Upright Porcupine, the Mighty Puma, the Fearless Bear and the Giant Snake. She also gave them five magic wands for their protection: one of turquoise, one of white shell, one of haliotis shell, one of black stone and one of red stone. The offspring said goodbye to their parents and grandmother, Changing Woman, and set out on the dangerous journey.

As they traveled, they were sighted by the Plains People. They were a large tribe, People of the Big Rabbit Bush. The travelers decided to rest for a while, and on the second night two young men visited the camp. One found fancy in one of their young girls and asked her to marry him. Eventually the people consented, since the young woman wanted to.

When the group was ready to move on, the young man wanted his wife to stay with him in his tribe. But, the travelers wanted him to go with them, and they prevailed. By the time they were ready to leave, four more young men had found wives among the travelers, and all were convinced to join in the journey.

On the first night after resuming their journey, a great wind came up. Fearless Bear became agitated. Looking out over the plain he observed some of the men of the group they had stayed with for a couple of days. When morning arrived, they discovered that the young men who had married their daughters were now missing.

The next night as they made camp, Fearless Bear became agitated again. The third night when they stopped for the night, again Fearless Bear became restless. When they were finally out of the valley of the people that they had spent a couple of days with, Fearless Bear seemed to be calm.

They were becoming very thirsty and they decided to try one of the magic wands Changing Woman had given them. Sure enough, as they forced it into the ground, a spring appeared and they had water. When they tasted the water, it was bitter, but it was water and that is how the clan got its name, Bitter Water clan or Bitter Water People.

When looking for a place to camp for the night, they came upon a group of people that seemed very much like themselves. They explained that they were the Coyote People, but the Navajo called them the Coyote Spring People. For four days they stayed among the Coyote Spring People. They were getting along well and the travelers asked the Coyote Spring People to join them on their journey to the east.

The next day, they all left for the east but the Coyote Spring People warned them that they would find no water for two days. Don't worry, the travelers said, we have ways. The second day they were getting very thirsty so they stopped and decided to try the magic wand again. With the white-shell wand, they found water but it was muddy water. They had their fill of muddy water, and so that is how the Mud clan got its name.

By noon the next day, they were thirsty again as they were traveling across the desert. This time they tried the haliotis wand and were successful in finding water, but it was salty, alkaline water. And that is how the Alkaline Water clan got its name.

The next day, by noon they were thirsty again and tried the Black Stone wand. With it, they found water—fine, clear water. All drank except two, one youth and a maiden whose people had carried the wand. When the girl was asked why they didn't drink, she did not answer, just stood there with arms crossed under her dress. This is why her clan is called the Close to Her Body clan.

As they traveled day after day, food was becoming harder to find. The Mighty Puma caught a deer, and Fearless Bear caught some rabbits, but Gentle Deer only gave them companionship. The Great Snake and Upright Porcupine were a chore and they decided to set them free east of

San Francisco Peaks, and that explains why there are so many snakes and porcupines in that area.

They had now reached a place where the present-day Hopis live. They camped there and tried hunting. They learned to use the deer hide as a decoy just in time, because the weather was cold and the deer hides provided warmth.

They were getting very weary and moving quite slow. They started to argue about whether to push on or stop until after winter, and whether the people they sought were really there. So, they split and some moved on and some waited until spring.

The ones that did not travel on became worried about the ones who had kept traveling. They sent out scouts, but the scouts did not return. So, they sent a second pair of scouts. They did not find the first two, but they found where the travelers had split into two groups. The Jicarilla Apaches are believed to have descended from one of the two lost bands, and the Navajo have visited them often. The other lost band seemed to have vanished.

The two scouts were giving up hope of finding their lost tribesmen. They even feared they were lost themselves. When looking for a valley for refuge, they came upon the San Juan River, where by chance they came upon the Navajo Nation they had been searching for. These two scouts were the two bedraggled strangers who stumbled into camp during the ceremony that the aged and feeble Chief Big Knee held to try to restore his youth.

In the spring, the travelers started out again. Before long, one group decided they had traveled as far as they could go and stopped by a tree. This group would thereafter be called the Clumped Tree clan. Another group called it quits and the Gentle Deer stayed with them. They would be called Deer Spring People or Deer Spring clan.

Eventually, the remaining travelers arrived at the place they had set out for and with gladness became part of that group. They were still in possession of Fearless Bear, but they knew he would not be happy there so they set him free. You will still find his offspring in the White Spruce Mountains.

As time went on, other groups became clans of the Navajo tribe and the Navajo people increased their numbers and their strength from within. Their existence as a tribe was secure, and to this day they still flourish on the surface of the fifth world.

This chapter is a very condensed version of the Navajo creation story as recorded in Paul G. Zolbrod's book *Diné Bahane' — The Navajo Creation Story*, which tells the story in much greater detail.

CHAPTER 9

Sorrow, Tragedy and a Broken Heart

For a while, during my school years at the College of Ganado, my husband and I and our babies lived with my husband's mother. After I graduated from the College of Ganado, I got a job through the tribal chapter house going door to door as a census taker; there weren't many opportunities for a nurse's aide on the reservation at that time. After some period of time, my mom and stepdad had moved to Parker, Arizona, where my stepdad was working in field irrigation.

My husband got a job as a heavy equipment operator in Parker, so off to Parker he, I and our five daughters went. I got a job at the local school cafeteria, but also applied for a nurse's aide position at Parker Regional Hospital. I was hired, so I now had my first opportunity to put my nurse's aide degree to work. I was excited to be working in the medical field and even more excited when my next baby arrived at the Lake Havasu Hospital. Finally, after five daughters, I now had a son.

By the time we moved back to Cornfields, my marriage was getting rocky due to my husband's extra-curricular activities.

Back on the reservation, I got a job managing the Exxon station and a small store for the lady who owned it. That was not a full-time job, and soon I applied for work at Hubbell's Trading Post, where I waited on customers interested in Navajo rugs or jewelry.

While working at the Exxon station, a young man who had just graduated from high school came in looking for a job and I hired him. That young man was Manley.

I would soon separate from my meandering husband, and I would eventually start doing things outside of work with Manley. He eventually became my common-law husband. While I did not have a legal divorce yet when I started doing social things with Manley, I was separated from my husband. So, while I worked long hours, my common-law husband would get the kiddies ready for school and see to it that the ones who had not started school had a babysitter—often my sister Geneva.

Government commodities.

It was sometimes hard making the dollars stretch with a family of seven growing children, but the government commodities helped fill the void. Often times, if our supply ran short and a family member had extra, they would share. The processed cheese was a favorite with the children and it was reasonably healthy.

By this time, my mom and stepdad had moved back to Sunrise. This was also about the time that my mom decided she'd had enough of her husband's abuse and drinking, so she separated from him. She also had started having severe headaches around this time. It probably wasn't too long after that when my stepdad was found dead in his truck, having frozen to death after falling into a drunken stupor.

My mom only had the shack that my stepdad had built at Cornfields to live in. There was no electricity and no running water, and my family was living with her, so my sister Jessie and I made application at the Chapter House to have a new house built for her. It was approved and built. Mom's new house had three bedrooms, and electricity and running water. Not long after this, Mom's headaches and dementia got so bad that she moved to a nursing home in Chinle.

Mom's headaches were becoming worse and worse, and finally the health care system on the Reservation had her transferred by airplane to St. Joseph's Hospital in Phoenix, Arizona. The plane was just big enough for a stretcher and a nurse in the back of the plane. I rode along in the co-pilot's position. All was going well until the nurse shouted that Mom had stopped breathing. I was over the seat and to the back of the plane in a flash, as the pilot yelled at me for endangering the flight by throwing off the balance of the plane. We got Mom breathing again, and we soon landed at St. Joseph's hospital.

For all practical purposes, I lived at St. Joseph's Hospital in Phoenix so that I could be with Mom until she was discharged. Following her surgery, where her skull was opened up so that a blood vessel could be repaired, she had no memory. She didn't recognize anybody. For four or five months I sat with her as much as I could, often sleeping in the recliner in her room.

Mom would often say, "Who are you? Why are you in my room? Go away!" Week after week, I waited. Then one day, she awoke from a nap, looked at me, and said, "Verna, is that you?" With tears of joy in my eyes, I crawled into bed with her and held her. Finally, my Mom was back.

When Mom was released from the hospital, she was transferred back to the nursing home in Chinle, and I returned to the reservation where I could be with my family and still take care of Mom. We were living at her new house, and on weekends we would bring her home to be with us.

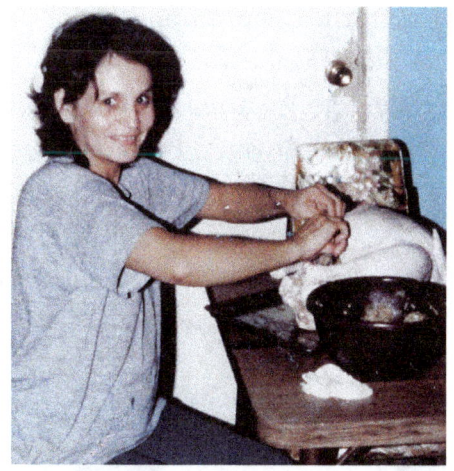

Mom's house at Cornfields. I (Verna) am stuffing a turkey in preparation for bringing Mom home from the nursing home for Thanksgiving.

I was working full-time at Hubbell Trading Post and through the tribal chapter house I got a job as a census taker that I would do on my days off work at Hubbell.

We took care of Mom as best we could for several years, but she was failing. After she passed, I was about to be blind-sided by a devastating incident in my personal life.

In the Navajo tradition the woman owns the hogan which is built on land set aside for her by her family. She owns the children and they belong to her clan. She owns the sheep and other livestock, as well as the product of her livestock. She also owns her jewelry and the blankets she has woven, as well as the income from the sale of any of her property. So, the woman who has given birth to the children, like Changing Woman did with the original Navajo, owns the property described so she can take care of the children and provide what they need, like Changing Woman did for the Navajos when they moved to their new home in the southwest.

The man owns what his family gives him and anything that he has saved, and made or produced for himself. Gary Witherspoon, in his book *Navajo Kinship and Marriage,* writes: "At best, a father is a helpful friend, a good teacher, and a strong disciplinarian; at worst, he is a potential enemy, an undependable friend, or an unreliable ally." Does that come from the creation story where Father Sun at first denied his children but in the end gave them assistance? Probably.

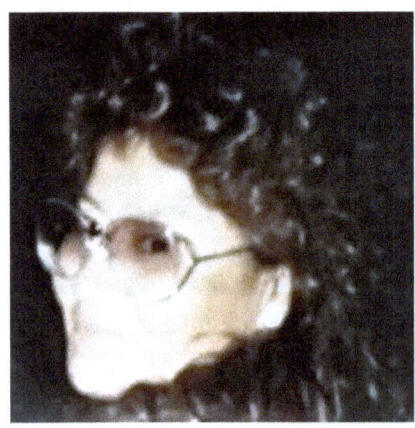

My (Verna's) sister Jessie.

After Mom passed, according to Navajo tradition, her house should have gone to her oldest daughter, Jessie. But Jessie had her own home with her family in Chinle, and really wasn't interested in moving back to Cornfields. That put me in line to have the house next, but I had plans to make my home in Phoenix.

Jessie suggested that she and I share the house so we could use it when we visited Cornfields. So, that is what we did for several years. My possessions were there because we had lived there during Mom's waning years. After Mom's passing, my family and I made the decision to permanently make our home in Phoenix and with my introduction during my Mom's surgery and recovery, I was able to get hired at St. Joseph's Hospital.

We would often visit Cornfields on weekends and stay at Mom's house, now Jessie and my house. Probably five or so years after Mom passed, tragedy struck.

When Franklin D. Roosevelt became president, a relief work program for unemployed young men was started called the Civilian Conservation Corps (CCC). Due to Indians' objection to the militaristic style of the CCC camps, a program just for Indians was started in 1933 called Indian Emergency Conservation Work (ICEW).

It was this program that built the fairgrounds at Window Rock for the Navajo Nation Fair. Jessie loved the Navajo Nation Fair, with all the pageantry, singing and dancing. On the way home after the evening perfor-

Navajo Fair in the early days.

mance at the fair, Jessie's son was driving and she was in the backseat with the youngsters. Out of the blue, a drunk driver roared up behind them, running into the rear of their car and causing the car to careen out of control. My dear sister Jessie was killed instantly.

When I got the news, I was devastated. My big sister, my idol, the sister I had followed to Intermountain Indian School, the sister with whom I had shared the agony of our stepdad's abuse, was gone. With a sad heart, I moved my possessions into a rented storage unit and headed for the Reservation to help Jessie's family. With all that was going on and with not enough income to go around, I defaulted on my storage unit lease and lost all my belongings. (Since Jesse's death, I have had no desire to visit the Navajo Nation Fair.)

After Jessie's passing, Navajo tradition would dictate that the house now belonged to me, since I was next in line. The older members of the family would often wonder out loud when I was going to move back to the Reservation and live in "my" house. Perhaps you have to be Navajo to understand how our families tend to stick together and take care of each other. I had no desire to move back to the Reservation; my home was in Phoenix, but I did like having a place to stay when I visited family.

On one trip to stay at my house, I was surprised to find that the key I had in my pocket did not work. Someone had drilled out the locks and changed them. Who would do that? They knew it was my house. I was hurt. Was I being disowned? Was it because I was only half Navajo? Did they think of me as a half-breed? Was it because I was becoming successful? Did they think they deserved the house more than me? I thought my family loved me.

Before I returned to Phoenix, I made it known to family members that I would be back to retrieve my belongings that were locked in the house and the culprit would have to reveal himself or herself and unlock the door for me. But it would get worse; my youngest sister, who was not a part of it, did not approve of what she saw happening and told me that they had removed my belongings from the house and burned them. It wasn't that there were a lot of possessions of value stored at the house. What I mourned was the loss of the sentimental mementos: the things my kids made for me in school, my family photos and documents, the Navajo corn grinding stone, my Navajo brush, the silver bracelet that had originally belonged to my grandma and had been handed down to Mom and then to me. Those were treasures that could not be replaced.

I don't know what my family was thinking, but I was deeply hurt by what they did. I felt left out and pushed away, and that I didn't belong and wasn't respected as the oldest sister. To this day, I am still left out, and it hurts. I have forgiven them, but I will never forget.

While my Navajo family rejected me, my white family accepted and supported me. One of my white brothers said, "Let it go, Sis. You have family here that loves you." I also have my children, grandchildren and great grandchildren. Yes, I am a great-grandma, and I love all of them with all my heart.

My family: Back row, left to right: Vernadine, Harry, Denise, Harranna, Veronica and Angela Front row, left to right: Veranna, Me (Verna) Manda and Mandy

CHAPTER 10

The Power Behind the Fighting

On cold winter evenings, Grandma told us about how raiding parties would attack Navajo homes and destroy things while stealing livestock and especially young women and girls. She said they had to be always on guard. She also talked about how many Navajo warriors were killed as the government took more and more of their land.

Grandma's stories were bits and pieces of the actual history of my ancestors, so these next two chapters are our attempts to piece together the story of survival in the years leading up to the Long Walk. The history that we attempt to retell in this chapter comes from various sources, and sometimes the dates and even the events don't agree, but we have done our best to weave it together, knowing that there will be errors. The story is worth telling, so please be lenient in judging our version.

Even when Spain controlled Navajo territory, which ended with Mexican independence in 1821, Navajo people and the New Mexican people were attacking each other. With independence, the Governor of New Mexico came up with a plan for settling the Navajo in Pueblos and converting them to the Catholic religion. The Navajo rejected that proposal and renewed the fight. The Governor then led an expedition of 1,500 troops into Navajo territory, killing some 33 Navajos and taking about the same number of prisoners. In response, the Navajos raided Socorro and moved on to Tome, Albuquerque, and made it almost to Santa Fe. These raids continued until 1848.

In 1845, Democrat James Polk became the President of the United States. His goal was to expand United States territory in the southwest.

After Mexico refused Polk's offer to purchase the territory, the war between the United States and the Republic of Mexico was declared in 1846. Navajo territory, Grandma told us, had been part of Mexico until the Treaty of Guadalupe Hidalgo between the United States and the Republic of Mexico that ended the war

President James Polk

between Mexico and the United States in 1848. This treaty gave what is now California, half of New Mexico, most of Arizona, Nevada, Utah and Colorado to the United States.

President Polk was a supporter of Andrew Jackson, who was a slavery proponent and an expansionist. In his last message to Congress on December 5, 1848, Polk announced the gold strike in the newly acquired territory which triggered a mass exodus to California; which would make life extremely difficult for my ancestors, the Navajo tribe.

There was a good market for Navajo slaves in New Mexico, because even though the Mexican Republic had abolished the slavery of black people in 1834, they did not abolish Indian slavery. The Utes and the New Mexicans were the most frequent raiders but occasionally the Zuni, Kiowa, Comanche, Pueblo and Apache raided our Navajo settlements. Often the raiding parties would put the stolen girls on the slave block on their way home to their own tribes. It was easy money. Even the family of the young John Hubbell, who had become a friend to the Navajo in later years, Grandma told us, had owned Navajo slaves.

Livestock (sheep, goats, cattle and horses) and the grains that they raised in their fields (primarily corn) was the wealth of my ancestors at that time. So raiding parties would make off with the livestock that they could accumulate on raids and would then consider it their property. Obviously, especially for young warrior types, revenge was in order, both in order to retrieve or enhance property but most importantly, to retrieve their daughters, sisters, wives or girlfriends and return them to their families, if they

Chief Narbona

could get there before they were sold on the slave block.

Grandma told us about how United States soldiers had killed Narbona in 1849. Narbona was Manuelito's father-in-law and was in his eighties when the United States was making more and more demands on his followers. He apparently thought that he could make the American soldiers happy by complying with their demands but it was not working. He did not want war.

At a meeting between the Navajo Chief Narbona, who was accompanied by his followers, and Colonel John Washington, with the soldiers he commanded, chaos broke out amongst the Navajo warriors, instigated by Sandoval. Sandoval was the headman of the Canoncito band, an enemy of Narbona's band, partly because he had been forced by the soldiers to lead a raiding party against the Navajo. Sandoval explained the terms of the council they were just completing, and in so doing he accused the warriors of starting the fight which angered the Navajo warriors.

Noise and anger grew and a New Mexican loudly accused a Navajo of having stolen his horse. Narbona tried to calm things down, but when Colonel Washington demanded that the Navajo give up his horse to the New Mexican, the Navajo jumped on his horse and galloped away. Washington then demanded that the Navajo give up another horse and warned them that if they didn't, his soldiers would open fire.

The meeting was in chaos and the soldiers raised their guns. Narbona stood holding the reins of his horse and trying to calm his warriors down when Washington gave the command to fire. After the smoke cleared, Narbona and seven other warriors lay dead and Narbona's pony ran away.

Manuelito became the new Chief of the Chuska Navajo and vowed revenge for his father-in-law's killing.

Vice President Millard Fillmore, also a Democrat, became President of the United States in 1850, after President Taylor died in office. It was under Fillmore's administration that Fort Defiance was established in 1851 by Colonel Edwin Sumner to create a military presence in Navajo territory (never mind that the fort was established on the grazing grounds of Navajo War Chief Manuelito).

The raids by the Utes continued and Manuelito was probably right when he said that they were being encouraged by the New Mexicans, who wanted the Navajo slave trade to continue. They were probably also encouraged by the United States, who wanted the land, and by the Mormons through the Ute Indian agent Kit Carson. My ancestors, the Navajo, were starving because of this.

Some, like Zarcillos Largos, were arguing for peace and some, like Manuelito, were arguing for war. When the Navajo protested the raids to their agent, Brooks, they were told that the Utes were from Colorado territory and their agent was Kit Carson, so it was beyond his jurisdiction. What it boiled down to was the Utes and the New Mexicans created a constant threat and the Americans cooperated with these attackers.

As a result of the drought, grass was becoming scarce and Manuelito's herd was moved to the grassy area at Ewell's camp, but Major Brooks demanded that he remove them. The Major also sent Largos, who was the peace headman, and his soldiers to tell Manuelito to keep his herd off the grassy area. Manuelito and Largos rode back to the fort to talk to Major Brooks. Manuelito said that he would move his herd but Major Brooks' nasty attitude made Manuelito angry, so he didn't remove his herd.

He became even angrier when Major Brooks decided that Largos was head chief of the Navajos. Brooks demanded that Manuelito and Largos gather up the sheep that the New Mexicans claimed had been stolen from them and return them to the fort. Without Manuelito's help, Largos did that and peace prevailed for a while.

Agent Brooks summoned Manuelito to the fort and demanded that he remove his herd from the grassy area and Manuelito, while saying that he did not want war, refused to remove his herd. Brooks declared the Navajo were now enemies of the United States government after this refusal. Both were angry and Brooks took matters into his own hands and had his soldiers shoot Manuelito's herd of cattle.

The Navajos salvaged as much as they could of the meat and hides and then called a meeting at Chinle. Manuelito wanted war, Largos wanted peace, and Largos prevailed. The meeting ended with the decision that Manuelito would convince Agent Brooks to reimburse him for his herd. Major Brooks refused Manuelito's request; the very idea that Manuelito would even ask made him even angrier.

Rumors were spreading that Agent Brooks was planning to take even more of the Navajo land, and before long, soldiers started cutting hay on Navajo land. When the Navajo saw what was happening, they waited until the soldiers were asleep in their tents and attacked. While they did very little damage, they frightened the soldiers enough that they returned to the fort with what little hay they had already cut. While on the one hand the Navajo were trying to maintain peace, there was an element that could not ignore what was being done to them and they were causing trouble like the hay field attack.

The Navajo leaders decided to appeal to a higher level in an effort to get payment for Manuelito's herd. So, off to Albuquerque they rode to deliver a letter to New Mexico Territory's Governor Rencher. They were not allowed to see the governor and it is unlikely that his aides ever delivered the letter to him.

After Agent Brooks' black slave was murdered, the Fort demanded that the Navajo produce the murderer. Again, in an effort to maintain peace, the Navajo produced a dead body, but it was determined that this body had just died and could not be the actual murderer and war was declared against the Navajo.

Retaliation Begins

On September 9, 1858, Colonel Miles led five companies toward Canyon de Chelly. The first night they camped at Ewell's camp. One group then headed for Chinle wash where they burned fields and damaged many hogans. There were a few deaths on each side, but the Navajo lost 6,000 sheep. Another group attacked Largo's area, but Largo had made a deal for guns in preparation for an attack and was able to repel the soldiers. The soldiers reported that Largo was dead, but he was very much alive.

About three weeks later, Colonel Miles attacked Manuelito's area at Chuska Valley. Manuelito was not prepared and the soldiers got 5,000 sheep, 79 horses and destroyed fields and hogans. Ten Navajo and one soldier were killed in the fighting.

Another treaty was signed in late 1858 that made the Navajo tribe responsible for the actions of any of its members. The treaty also said that the United States could build posts on Navajo land at any time, and gave most of the Navajo's good land to the United States. The Navajo were directed to select one chief for the whole tribe. Manuelito would not sign this treaty.

The government forced the tribe to accept Huerro as their head chief. This put Huerro, who was the head blacksmith at Fort Defiance, in a difficult position. With the poor land left to the Navajo after this treaty, there is no way they could survive.

Zarcillos Largos called a council to meet northeast of Chinle Wash and a thousand or more Navajo attended. Largos argued for peace and Ganado Mucho agreed with him, while Manuelito argued for war. This time, no decision was reached.

Some 4,000 Navajo lived in the area now claimed by the United States and the majority moved but not all.

Raids Continue

The Utes continued their raids against the Navajo, so a council was called between the Utes and the Navajo. Kit Carson represented the Mauhache Utes, but it was the Southern Utes that did most of the raiding so the decision to all live together in peace did not stop the raiding.

From 1853 to 1861 the United States was led by Presidents Pierce and Buchanan, both Democrats in favor of slavery, so they were of no help in stopping the Navajo slave trade. The United States thought they had achieved peace, so they decided to distribute some treaty goods to the Navajo that they had been holding.

The Navajo were starving and Manuelito acted by raiding Ute and New Mexican settlements. The United States retaliated by sending an expedition under the command of Major John Simonson against the Navajo. The United States claimed that the Navajos owed the New Mexicans $14,000. The Navajos started making some payments but would not sign an agreement saying that they owed the amount. Ganado Mucho tried to cooperate with the United States agents, but finally he'd had enough.

In January, Navajos under Manuelito and Huerro led 200 warriors against the soldier's hay camp. They burned haystacks and ran off some of the cattle but the soldiers returned gunfire and the warriors had to back off.

One last peace mission failed and the Navajo tribe was at war. Manuelito and his troops encircled the vulnerable Fort Defiance. One thousand warriors were ready and waiting for Manuelito's signal to attack. The attack caught the soldiers off guard and the battle went on for about an hour before the soldiers got the upper hand and Manuelito signaled defeat. Seven Navajo warriors had been killed.

Following the attack, Captain Shepard wanted to abandon the fort but he was overruled by his superiors. That spring the Utes and the New Mexicans attacked the Navajo and captured thirty-five children for the slave block. The Navajo had to constantly watch for attacks from the Utes, the New Mexicans and the U.S. soldiers. That fall United States soldiers tried to force the Navajo to west of Fort Defiance, and Zarcillos Largos was killed in raids by the New Mexicans and the Zuni.

Request for Peace

By the end of 1860, a Navajo delegation asked for peace because they were starving and freezing. The United States called a general peace conference for the following January, but they were more concerned about the approaching Civil War than they were about the Navajo. To cement their friendship, the Navajo and the whites decided to participate in horse races at Fort Wingate. Manuelito had the fastest horse and was expected to win but someone had slashed one of the reins of Manuelito's horse. As a result, the horse veered off the track and he lost.

The all-white panel of judges laughed at Manuelito, and the Navajo were angry. When they protested, the soldiers opened fire, killing fifteen Navajo, mostly women and children. This caused friendly relations to evaporate completely.

Before long, as a result of the value of Navajo slaves, raiding parties included Utes, New Mexicans, Zuni, Kiowa, and Comanche.

A New Commander Named to Deal with the Navajo People

Because of promotions in the Civil War, General James H. Carleton took over the command that dealt with the Navajo. Carleton was born in 1814 in the area that would become the state of Maine. His father died when he was fifteen, and young Carleton dreamed of becoming a writer like Charles Dickens, who was about his same age. But his writing career was floundering and when, with John Quincy Adams as the president of the United States, the northern border between the United States and England's territory became an issue, Carleton was drawn into military service with the Maine militia.

General James H. Carleton

During this time (from 1830-1850), an ethnic cleansing and forced displacement of approximately 60,000 people of the "Five Civilized Tribes" knows as the Trail of Tears was underway, led by the United States government. As part of this "Indian removal," members of the Cherokee, Muscogee (Creek), Seminole, Chickasaw, and Choctaw nations were forcibly removed from their ancestral homelands in the Southeastern United States to newly designated Indian Territory west of the Mississippi River after the passage of the Indian Removal Act in 1830. The Cherokee removal in 1838 (the last forced removal east of the Mississippi) was culminated by the discovery of gold near Dahlonega, Georgia, in 1828, resulting in the Georgia Gold Rush.

Carleton was praised for taking command of the troops when no one else was available. This drew the attention of Secretary of War Poinsett, who asked him to come to Washington to be tested for a commission. He was commissioned as a lieutenant in the U.S. Army in 1839, during the Aroostook War, and took part in the Mexican-American War.

Within a few weeks after Carleton's arrival at Fort Leavenworth from Fort Croghan in 1841, he found himself in serious trouble. A full year before, at Fort Gibson, he had become quite friendly with Lieutenant Wickliffe of his own regiment, the 1st Dragoons. Early in December, 1842, Wickliffe shot and killed a squatter living near the post. He was duly ordered into arrest by Lieutenant Colonel Richard Mason, the Post Commander, but shortly afterward he broke his arrest and disappeared.

A year later Colonel Mason suddenly preferred charges against Carleton, who had been Post Adjutant at the time of Wickliffe's disappearance. Mason accused Carleton of having deliberately falsified the morning report so that Wickliffe's absence was not discovered until he was safely away. Mason piled on other charges until it appeared that Carleton was a scoundrel who was unfit to associate with officers and gentlemen.

A General Court-martial, the highest form of military court, duly met at Fort Gibson, shortly before Christmas, 1843, and pondered the evidence for several weeks. Carleton's defense was a categorical denial of all of the specifications, and an accusation that Mason was motivated by spite the necessity of finding a "goat." The charges were such that conviction made dismissal from the service mandatory—no other sentence was legally permissible. Nevertheless, the court, after finding Carleton guilty and sentencing him to be dismissed from the service, appended to the record of the trial a strong recommendation for clemency!

It would seem that there was more to the case than appeared openly in the record of the trial, and evidently the President of the United States was of the same opinion, for John Tyler commuted the sentence to the purely nominal one of suspension from command for six months without pay. A slap on the wrist, by way of punishment! *(From the official record of the court martial, furnished by the National Archives)*

Texas Annexed

In 1845, Texas was annexed by the United States, and Texas claimed territory all the way to the Rio Grande River. Mexico disagreed, and recognized neither its independence nor its boundaries. President Polk tried to settle the dispute diplomatically and offered $5 million dollars for New Mexico or $25 million dollars for both New Mexico and California. Both offers were rejected. When Mexican troops crossed the Rio Grande, President Polk considered it an act of war and ordered General Zachary Taylor to prepare accordingly.

Lieutenant Carleton, still stationed at Fort Leavenworth, was appointed Assistant Inspector General and ordered to proceed to San Antonio in preparation for a march to the Rio Grande. With his literary skill, Carleton recorded the activities of the army.

The U.S. believed that General Santa Anna, the 8th President of Mexico, led an army of 20,000 troops and this idea was reinforced when he confidently sent a message to General Zachary Taylor asking him to surrender. Taylor refused and the war began on April 24, 1846.

The Battle of Bueno Visto started during a violent thunderstorm on February 22, 1847. Initially it appeared that the Mexicans had the advantage, but when General Taylor and Colonel Jefferson Davis's troops arrived, the Mexicans were forced to retreat. Fighting was fierce the first day. When daylight arrived the second morning, the American army discovered that the Mexicans had fled and that they had won the battle. James Carleton was involved in this one-day fight, not by doing any actual fighting but through his post as adjutant general from whom all orders flowed.

The Battle of Buena Vista marked a turning point in the war, because Santa Anna decided to attack Taylor, but did not reinforce Vera Cruz, a key Mexican beachhead. This battle lasted for 20 days, from March 9-29, 1847, and ended with the surrender and occupation of the city. This paved the way for General Winfield Scott to lead the march on Mexico City, where he raised the American flag of the Hall of Montezuma.

The Treaty of Guadalupe Hidalgo, signed on February 2, 1848, officially ended the war between the United States and Mexico. By its terms, Mexico ceded 55 percent of its territory, including the present-day states of California, Nevada, Utah, New Mexico, most of Arizona and Colorado, and parts of Oklahoma, Kansas, and Wyoming.

A Show of Military Might

In 1851, President Fillmore's Secretary of War, Charles Conrad, assigned Colonel Edwin Vose Sumner to command the 9th Military District, which included New Mexico and Arizona. Among other things, Conrad's orders were to organize expeditions against the Navajo, the Utes and the Apaches and make them "feel the power" of the United States. Sumner's aim was to awe the Indians with a show of military might. He adopted the scorched earth policy and threatened to destroy all the Navajo grain if they didn't behave like he wanted them to.

James Carleton supported this mission, and his main duty was to save the government money. Five forts were built, with Fort Union being the main supply base. On August 17, 1851, troops marched into Arizona to build the first fort there—Fort Defiance.

Fort Defiance painted by Seth Eastman.

In 1852, Carleton was in command of Fort Union and had been ordered by Colonel Sumner, the chief authority in New Mexico, to march his company of soldiers toward Bosque Redondo. They were to open communications with the Mescalero Apache. Carleton did not encounter any Indians on this march, but he saw the area where he would send the Navajo in the near future.

In the summer of 1852, Colonel Sumner led an expedition against the Navajo into Canyon de Chelly, only to be repulsed by boulders rolled off the cliffs onto the soldiers below. In February of 1854, the Indians attacked the soldiers near Taos, New Mexico. Major Carleton, who was stationed in Albuquerque, headed to Taos with his troops. All troops were mobilized and they went after the attackers, but the Indians made the pursuit so difficult the soldiers gave up. One of these companies was led by Colonel Christopher Carson.

Much of the sequence of events in this chapter that supplemented my memory, since it has been more than six decades since Grandma's stories, came from Sharon Leslie Gearhart's book *Seasons of the Enemies,* Aurora Hunt's book, *James H. Carleton, Frontier Dragoon* and Tom Dunlay's book *Kit Carson and the Indians.*

Canyon de Chelly National Monument, showing Spider Rock.

CHAPTER 11

Should We Blame Kit Carson?

The name Kit Carson does not generate admiration among my Navajo ancestors for many reasons. Exactly who was this Christopher "Kit" Carson? In many ways his life mirrored that of Andrew Jackson who was born forty years before Kit came into the world. The glaring difference between these two men was education, Jackson had a formal education and became a lawyer, while Carson was essentially illiterate. (This makes me suspect that Kit's writings were done by someone else.)

Christopher "Kit" Carson

Kit Carson was born in Kentucky on Christmas Eve 1809. When he was a year old, his family moved to Boone's Lick, Missouri, where they settled on land owned by Daniel Boone's sons. When Kit was eight years old, his father was killed by a falling tree limb. After four years as a widow, his mother married Joseph Martin. Kit did not get along well with his step-father.

As a teenager Kit was apprenticed to a saddle maker. At age sixteen, he'd had enough of saddle making and left to become a mountain man and trapper in the West. Carson lived the conflict between the Indians and the Anglos, who were invading their way of life, for about 16 years while working as a trapper and providing beaver pelts for the beaver hat industry.

That took him into the territory of the mountain tribes, and he encountered the Blackfeet, Flathead, Shoshone, Crow, Nez Perce and Utes. Some of these meetings were friendly, while others were not. Stories of trappers' encounters with Indians were popular reading back east. The ten-cent novels thrived on these stories and Carson's stories made him famous throughout the United States. Tales of his exploits appeared in government reports, dime novels, newspaper accounts, and were spread through word of mouth. Others capitalized on this fame and published their own, often times graphically violent, Kit Carson stories (fictional or not).

These stories portrayed Kit Carson as a ruthless Indian fighter, which was a total exaggeration. Yes, he defended himself, especially against the hostile Blackfeet Indians, when necessary but he also spent winters living with the various Indian tribes.

In 1835, Carson married Wannibe (Singing Grass). Carson was forced to fight a duel with a French trapper, Chouinard, in order to win Waanibe's hand in marriage. Carson won but had a narrow escape — the trapper's bullet singed his hair.

They had a daughter, Adaline, and then unfortunately Wannibe died giving birth to their second daughter (circa 1839). In 1841, Kit remarried, perhaps because he needed someone to care for his young daughters. This time, he married Making-Out-Road, a Cheyenne. They were only together a short time before Making-Out-Road divorced him in the way of her people by putting Adaline and all of Carson's property outside of her tent.

Carson soon realized his mountain man lifestyle was not suited to raising a daughter, so he took Adaline and her little sister to live with his sister Mary Ann Carson Rubey in St. Louis. Unfortunately, his youngest daughter died in 1843 after an accident.

About 1842, Carson met Josefa Jaramillo, the 13-year-old daughter of a prominent Mexican couple living in Taos. He married her on Feb. 6, 1843, after converting to Catholicism. He was more than twice her age at 33. They settled down permanently in Taos, New Mexico, and Adeline came to live with them there when she was a teenager. This marriage lasted for 25 years and they had eight children together, seven of which lived.

Carson's years as a trapper ended after about sixteen years, partly because the beaver were becoming scarce but also because fashion had changed and pelts were no longer sought after.

Carson and the Indians

Because of his experience as a trapper, Kit was knowledgeable about surviving in the mountains as well as dealing with the Indians they encountered. When John C. Fremont was commissioned for an expedition into the West, he hired Kit Carson as a scout. After having been away from his wife Josefa for a year scouting for Fremont he returned and started farming. He must have enjoyed the job of scouting because he told Fremont that if he went on any future expeditions he would scout for him. In 1845, when that opportunity arose, he sold his farming operation and signed on as Fremont's scout.

This expedition, as it turned out, was more than just the exploration that it had been commissioned for and this caused much controversy between the military, of which he was a part, and Fremont. There may have been a separate agreement between Fremont and President Polk because we know that President Polk wanted expansion of the United States all the way to the Pacific, and we know that President Polk commuted Fremont's sentence after he had been court-martialed for mutiny and insubordination.

The expedition was venturing into California, then controlled by Mexico, and into Oregon territory, then controlled by Great Britain, which was beyond the scope of their commission, but Fremont thought he had permission to seize California. As the expedition entered its final phases, Carson was given the assignment of delivering messages back and forth between Fremont on the west coast and President Polk in Washington. Carson liked those missions because he could squeeze in a short visit with his wife on the way.

On one of these missions President Polk gave Carson a lieutenant's commission as a reward for his service, but the commission was not confirmed by the senate because Fremont was being court-martialed. That didn't bother Carson much because he had never asked to be considered for a commission and really was not interested in a military career. Carson's reputation was being enhanced by Fremont's reports on his expeditions that gave glowing reviews of Kit's expertise and made him famous as a great scout.

This caught General William Tecumseh Sherman's attention and gave him a desire to meet Kit Carson. Perhaps he was disappointed when he met Carson because he described him as "a small, stoop-shouldered man, with reddish hair, freckled face, soft blue eyes, and nothing to indicate extraordinary courage and daring," as Tom Dunlay wrote in *Kit Carson and the Indians.*

In 1853, Carson was appointed Indian agent for the Mauche Utes, the Jicarilla Apache and the Taos Pueblo. He had not asked for this appointment but he accepted it and moved back to Taos, partly because he was given no agency to work out of, but also so Josefa could be closer to her family.

At this point, his wandering days were over. Taos was in New Mexico Territory, which included Arizona and southern Colorado. This assignment was probably difficult for Carson, we think, partly because he had lived with and communicated with the Indians for so long and he knew them.

In analyzing the things he wrote, Tom Dunlay in his book *Kit Carson and the Indians* gives the reader the impression that while Carson was part of the Manifest Destiny that was depriving the Indians of their traditional means of survival, he was sympathetic to them. While he was concerned for the safety of the settlers, he knew that the settlers were in large part to blame.

By 1857, the government's policy toward Indians went something like this: The Indians were to cease hostilities, give up their land claims and agree to live on designated reserves where they were expected to begin farming and herding. In return, the government would provide them with annuities which would be given to them in the form of goods or spent by the government on their "moral improvement and civilization." All liquor was to be barred from these reservations and all trade with whites would be regulated by the government.

One can easily understand that this was a bitter pill to be swallowed by people who for generations had been free, but their hunting grounds were gone and they were hungry. Keeping the Indians over which he was in charge satisfied with what the government was doing when he himself was not completely satisfied with how the government was doing it must have been difficult for Carson.

When the Indians were starving they would steal cattle and horses, this was especially true for the Utes and Jicarillas. Indians would show up at Carson's door because they were hungry and asking about the promises of supplies from the government. He could ask but he had no real power over the annuities, and he could not in good conscience send them away hungry. So, he would feed them with government funds if he had some at his disposal, and when that was gone from his own pocket.

When Carson was finished as Indian agent in 1861, just when the United States was about to fight a fearsome civil war, there was still no reservation and no agency, just hungry Indians who were being deprived of their way of life by the pressure of Anglo settlers. The Indians faced more than just the pressure from the settlers that was causing unrest in the new Mexican territory, there was also constant raiding primarily between the Navajo and the New Mexicans, and to a lesser extent between the Navajo and the Utes. It is impossible to know which party first started the raiding, but with no law or courts yet in existence in the territory, revenge was the way of settling scores.

While we have found no absolute proof, we are suspicious that it was the Navajo slave trade fostered by the New Mexicans that they inherited from Spanish Mexico that started the raiding. There was a ready market for Navajo slaves and any New Mexican that could afford one or more Navajo slaves had them, including the family of John Hubbell and even Kit Carson himself.

While African slaves were rare in New Mexico Territory, many of the Anglos who had migrated to the area came from slave states and were used to having slaves. So, with no kidnapping laws or courts to enforce them, the young Navajo warriors and their New Mexican counterparts engaged in raiding as a means of revenge. Ute raiders could often steal Navajo women and girls and have them sold for easy money before they made their way back to their tribe. The military at times tried to ensure peace but without much success.

To make things worse, gold was discovered in the western part of Kansas territory in the area that would soon become Colorado, increasing the pressure on the Utes by prospectors. This would eventually spill over into Navajo territory.

The United States government had no consistency with enforcement and sometimes was just plain cruel. (This is what we in 2023 at the writing of this book call Federal Indian Policy.)

Scientists were busy proving by scientific study that Indians were incapable, because of inherent inferiority, of mastering the complexities of civilized life. They were measuring skulls and coming to conclusions that the Indians were not worth saving. Because of this, Carson was afraid that the Indians would cease to exist unless they were put on a reservation and protected by military guards, so he favored reservations.

The status quo certainly wasn't working out well for the Indians. Complaints about how they were being treated more often than not ran up against a brick wall. Governor A.C. Hunt of Colorado is quoted as saying, "It is impossible to answer these complaints, for I know too well their justness; but as a true agent of the government I cannot admit the wrong, and I fear my attempted explanations but disgust the Indians instead of appeasing them."

At this point, the nation's attention was being shifted to saving the Union. When the Confederate Army launched an invasion of New Mexico, Kit Carson signed up to fight the Confederates and took some Utes with him. Carson was promoted to full colonel and commanded a regiment of Union soldiers.

Commander James Henry Carleton

While the soldiers were busy elsewhere, the Navajo and the Apache increased their raiding. In August of 1862, a California brigade of volunteer troops was sent to help drive the rebels out of New Mexico. That brigade was commanded by James Carleton. Shortly thereafter, Carleton was made Commander of the Department of New Mexico, a fateful occasion for the Navajo. While Carleton did not often engage in actual fighting, he commanded the action with Kit Carson as his principal field commander.

Once the rebels were driven out of New Mexico, the emphasis of the army turned to the Navajo who they considered their most troublesome Indian enemy. Colonel Edward Canby issued the orders for the attack on the Navajo just before he turned the command over to Commander Carleton.

James Henry Carleton, born in Maine in 1814, was an intellectual of sorts and did not have a high opinion of Indians. He is reported to have written that "an Indian is a more watchful and wary animal than a deer. He must be hunted with skill …", not an honorable opinion for a commander of the Department of New Mexico to have. As commander, Carleton had established Fort Sumner as a military post and he soon came up with the idea of housing the Indians, at first the Mescalero Apache, in what he thought would be a great area that the Indians could develop into an agricultural area under the watchful eye of Fort Sumner, Bosque Redondo. After all, the Mescalero Apache had been used to going there to trade anyway. By March of 1863, most of the Mescalero Apache were at Bosque Redondo, Arizona had become a separate territory, and they were now ready to concentrate on the Navajo.

Quoting from Tom Dunlay's book, *Kit Carson and the Indians*, Commander Carleton explained, "It may be set down as a rule that these Navajo Indians have long since passed that point when talking would be of any avail. They must be whipped and fear us before they will cease killing and robbing the people." Carleton thought Kit Carson was the man for that job.

Carson had other ideas and on February 3, 1863, he submitted his resignation. Carson had joined the army because he wanted to help defend New Mexico against the Confederates and now he wanted to go home.

Carson and Carleton had been friends of sorts for a long time, and Carson admired the Utes who were enemies of the Navajo. So, he really did not want to be the one to do it, but he seems to have thought that war against the Navajos was necessary, so he agreed to withdraw his resignation.

Two articles from the Santa Fe Gazette give us a window into the attitudes and the happenings at the time.

On June 27, 1863, a *Gazette* article reported that a party of Apaches and Utahs made a raid into Navajo country during which they killed ten Navajo and took thirty or forty women and children prisoner to be they supposed, "disposed of in the usual manner." Was slavery that "usual manner"?

On September 21, 1863, a *Gazette* article announced that Gov. Henry Connelly issued a proclamation to the people of New Mexico Territory to raise a regiment of volunteers to defend it against its enemies. He is quoted as saying, "Until the Navajos and Apaches are either subjugated or exterminated there will be no safety."

It seemed like everybody was against the Navajo.

Commander Canby had started the war against the Navajo even before the Civil War started, and Commander Carleton pretty much adopted Canby's plan to destroy or seize their crops while the Utes were seizing their livestock until they finally surrendered. Canby thought the only way to stop the raiding between the Navajo and the New Mexicans was to put the Navajo on a reservation.

On June 23, 1863, Brigadier General Carleton sent orders to Colonel Chavez and Colonel Carson authorizing war against the Navajo Indians in hopes that as a result "the people of New Mexico will become more secure in their persons and properties." Carleton claimed that he had told Barboncito and Delgadito [Navajo Chiefs] that the only way the soldiers could tell the difference between the peaceful Navajo and the raiding Navajo was for all the peaceful Navajo to come to Fort Wingate where they would be transported to Bosque Redondo, leaving only the raiding Navajo for the soldiers to fight. No Navajo went to Fort Wingate.

Carson Assumes Command

Kit Carson assumed his command on July 7, 1863, less than two weeks after the deadline that had been set for all Navajo to turn themselves in at Fort Wingate. Being friends with the Utes, Carson asked and was permitted to include 736 Utes in his fighting force. His orders were to kill any Navajo men they encountered and to take any women and children prisoner as they proceeded toward Ganado (then called Pueblo, Colorado) where they were to establish Fort Canby.

As they moved, the Utes would do most of the killing while the soldiers helped themselves to the Navajo's crops. When they arrived at Ganado, Carson did not like the site for his headquarters because there was no grass, no water and no timber so he established headquarters at Fort Defiance and renamed it Fort Canby.

While the actions of the more militant young Navajo were probably responsible for the raiding problem, the way the United States government chose to solve the problem was not only far from admirable but downright cruel. It seems obvious that Canby and Carleton were the brains behind this effort to move the Navajo to a reservation. We also know that Kit Carson didn't really want to be the one to carry it out, but he did. Carson was what we would call "street wise" today, but he did not have the intellectual background to stand up to his superiors. He oversaw the situation where the Navajo people were being assaulted from all directions and even though he was basically a kind person, it is difficult to forgive him for this.

War is always hell, but Carleton's campaign, while not the first time the scorched earth policy had been used, was especially brutal and destructive. On Carson's first move against the Navajo, he reported by letter to his superior that 70 acres of corn had been destroyed.

Later the same day he reported camping in wheat and corn fields with 15 acres of wheat being fed to the horses and 50 acres of corn being destroyed. They had seen two Indians and pursued them but only succeeded in capturing one horse. On another day he reported that eleven women and children had been captured as well as 100 sheep and goats.

Later that day he reported capturing two children and one horse as well as finding and destroying five acres of corn.

As the soldiers made their way from place to place in the Navajo's home country their mission was to kill Navajo men, capture women and children, destroy corn fields, wheat fields, peach orchards and even villages until the Navajo finally agreed to migrate to Bosque Redondo.

As winter approached, Carson asked for a two month leave of absence but his request was denied. Instead, he was ordered to lead his troops into Canyon de Chelly where many Navajo were hiding. The floor of the canyon with its fertile soil and abundant moisture was perfect for raising corn and growing peaches, but it was now winter. The Navajo people were in hiding in the canyon, and they were starving. Many were ready to surrender but they were afraid to approach the soldiers for fear of being killed.

Canyon de Chelly National Monument.

Finally, four brave Navajo men, despite fear of death, were able to let Carson know that there were many who were ready to surrender if they could do so safely. Arrangements were made, and most of the Navajo complied. By February, many of the starving Navajo had surrendered to the soldiers. Carson believed that the Indians now knew that there was no safe place to hide, that their struggle was hopeless, and that the government was not there to kill them but to take care of them if they would surrender.

According to researcher Frank McNitt 11,612 Navajo were sent to Bosque Redondo, 336 died enroute, 220 escaped, 20 were stolen, meaning only 8,846 actually arrived there. Obviously, these figures do not add up. What happened to the other 2,000?

On April 21, 1864, Carson resigned his command and left. He had not really wanted a military career yet a major portion of his life had been spent in military operations.

Since he had developed a reputation for being knowledgeable concerning Indian affairs, Senator James Doolittle, then Chairman of the Senate Committee on Indian Affairs, relied heavily on Carson's advice in dealing with Indian issues in the West. Tom Dunlay in *Kit Carson and the Indians* quotes Carson as telling Senator Doolittle that "nearly every instance of difficulties between the Indians and the whites arose from aggressiveness on the Indians by the whites." He described the Navajo as "the hardy, industrious agricultural Navajo" but thought the only answer was to put the Indians on reservations "with wise rules enforced by military power," and in so doing protecting the settlers from the Indians and the Indians from the "the reckless injustice of those outlaws of society ... whose criminality has too often been the means of rousing the Indians to thoughts of vengeance ...."

Doolittle continued his investigation by interviewing James Carleton who told him that the Indians were decreasing rapidly in numbers due to wars, alcohol abuse, venereal and other diseases and "the causes which the Almighty originates, when in their appointed time He wills that one race of men – as in races of lower animals – shall disappear off the face of the earth and give place to another race ... the red man is passing away!" He told Doolittle, "We have taken quite enough from the Indian."

Wise Man or Scoundrel?

Who was the wise man and who was the scoundrel? Was it the illiterate mountain man Kit Carson or the educated easterner James Carleton? We will leave the answer to the reader.

Carson's health was failing and he submitted his resignation from volunteer service in 1867. Within a year Carson's wife of 25 years, Josefa, died, probably from complications regarding child birth, leaving seven children and a husband on his death bed. Kit Carson died on May 23, 1868 when an aortic aneurysm burst killing him instantly.

Five days after Kit Carson's death, a conference was held regarding Bosque Redondo. The primary question to be answered: could the Navajo be trusted to not start raiding again if they were returned to their old lands?

Navajo raids were being blamed for the unrest and was the justification for war against them. So, what caused the raids? Was it competition and hatred between the various tribes? We know that certain tribes were always at war with one another, like the Utes and the Navajo. Or was it the encroachment on Navajo lands by settlement and by the government? Or was it the Navajo slave trade inherited from Mexico and Spain? Or was it because revenge was a common method of settling scores before real law was established?

Navajo Slave Trade

Juan Baptiste Laney, the Roman Catholic bishop of New Mexico, Arizona and Colorado for fourteen years is quoted as saying, "There are a good many Navajo captives among the Mexican families; they make the best servants. Some families abuse them, while others treat them like their own children. Most of the Mexican families have them; there are more than a thousand of them, perhaps two or three thousand.

Part of these captives have been taken in war by the Mexicans, and part have been purchased from the Indians, such as the Utes, who are constantly at war with the Navajos. These slaves have been bought and sold in this manner for years but of late the traffic has been greatly diminished through the agency of General Carleton and also in a certain degree through that of other persons."

Louis Kennon wrote,

> Am a resident of New Mexico; have been for twelve
> years last past; am a native of Georgia; am a physician by
> profession…I was in the service of the United States as act-
> ing assistant surgeon, and was stationed at Fort Defiance

in 1858…I think the number of Navajo captives held as slaves to be underestimated. I think there are from five to six thousand. I know of no family which can raise one hundred and fifty dollars but what purchases a Navajo slave, and many families own four or five. … I have been conversant with the institution of slavery in Georgia, but the system is worse here, there being no obligation resting on the owner to care for the slave when he becomes old or worthless … I think the system of Indian slavery is the origin of all the difficulties.

Some believe that the discovery of gold was the main reason for removing the Navajo. Others claim that the Navajo sided with the Confederacy in the Civil war, but neither of these claims seem credible. We believe that the Navajo slave trade and the resulting revenge raids were to blame.

Regardless of who or what was to blame, Changing Woman had told them that this was to be their home country, but now they had no choice. They were being starved into submission and were being made prisoners of the United States Government and being sent to a concentration camp called a reservation, Bosque Redondo. Grandmothers down through the generations have told their grandchildren the stories of what the white man's army did to their ancestors.

In the writing of this chapter we have relied heavily on the well-written and well-archived books, *Kit Carson and the Indians* by Tom Dunlay, *James H. Carleton Frontier Dragoon* by Aurora Hunt and *The Navajo Treaty 1868* by Bernhard Michaelis. We thank them for their efforts.

CHAPTER 12

The Long Walk

History Repeats Itself — Another Trail of Tears

My big sis, Jessie, would often get distracted and start playing Jacks or something when Grandma was telling stories, but Grandma's stories fascinated me. I fondly remember laying my head on Grandma's lap while she told us about how the Utes and the New Mexicans would steal little girls like me and sell them to the New Mexicans as slaves. It was scary, but I felt safe next to Grandma.

General James H. Carleton was military commander of New Mexico Territory, so he was in charge. He had a plan to get the Navajo people out of the way so the American settlers could have the land and explore for the gold and silver they thought was hidden in the mountainous areas. Despite the recommendation of the Board of Officers that the Bosque Redondo was not a good site for a reservation (Bosque Redondo had previously been a trading post established by the Spanish for trade with the Indian tribes), Carleton convinced President Lincoln to approve 13,000 acres to establish Fort Sumner.

Carleton's plan was to hunt down all the Navajo and put them on a reservation far away from Navajo territory. This wonderful new land, the Bosque Redondo Reservation, would be overseen by Fort Sumner. "We will be kind to them," Carleton said, "and teach their children how to read and write, teach them the arts of peace, and teach them the truths about Christianity." Carleton is also quoted as saying, "The only peace that will

107

come for the Navajo is if they will give up being nomads and live on a reservation and little by little, the Navajo would become a happy, contented people, and Navajo wars would be remembered only as something that belongs entirely to the past."

The Civil War was being fought during the time when Carleton assumed his post as military commander of the New Mexico Territory. The objectives of his command were to defend against confederate attacks, establish a mail route in the region and defeat the Navajo.

While Carleton was sitting in his headquarters, dreaming about the gold he would find in Navajo country, Colonel Christopher (Kit) Carson, known to the Navajo as Red Shirt, was given command of the troops assigned to do the job of removing the Navajo. Carleton moved his headquarters to Fort Defiance and renamed it Fort Canby.

Carson's heart was not in fighting the Indians, after all he had been married to two different Indian women, and he had resigned his post as Agent to the Utes to fight against the Confederates. Regardless, he obeyed the orders of his superior officer, especially because he remembered the trouble Fremont got into by disobeying orders.

In March of 1863, Carson's troops attacked the Mescalero Apaches. They surrendered and 400 were sent to Fort Sumner. By April the word was put out that there would be no peace until the Navajo joined the Mescalero Apaches, and the Navajo were given until July 20th to surrender.

The kidnapping of women and young girls was stepped up because of this, as the kidnappers could see that their source was about to disappear. There was big money in slaves for household help, farm labor and the sex trade in Mexico. These despicable men followed the troops and Kit Carson didn't object, partly because he thought being a slave might be better than going to Bosque Redondo. (In some ways, he might have been right in his thinking.)

Some of the Navajo were not leaving no matter what, while some were ready to surrender. Many knew that the Army was coming, so they fled west and went into hiding, often high in the mountainous areas. Others who waited for the soldiers to approach so they could surrender, were shot in the forehead without warning, regardless of their age. Kit Carson's one thousand troops were also out to destroy everything the Navajo could survive on, so they had no choice but to surrender.

Grandma told us stories about how the soldiers burned their hogans and all their food, clothing and belongings. She said they trampled and destroyed their corn fields and other crops, chopped down and burned the peach trees, and took the livestock for use at the fort or just killed the animals.

In August, four Navajo men went to Fort Defiance, located near what is now Window Rock, under a flag of truce. Their intent was to negotiate a surrender for themselves and about one hundred of their relatives. Instead of being heard, the four men were imprisoned and put to work cleaning the privy. When a soldier shot one of them, two others jumped the wall and ran. So much for the meaning of a flag of truce.

By the first week of September, only 51 Navajo had been sent to Bosque Redondo. General Carleton reported to New Mexico Headquarters writing, "This week [I] sent fifty-one Navajo Indians, men, women and children to Fort Sumner, at the Bosque Redondo, on the Pecos river, where, as I have before informed you, I have four hundred and twenty-five Mescalero Apaches held as prisoners."

Carson meanwhile gave the order to his troops that every Navajo man must die and the women and children were to be taken captive. He is quoted as saying, "Say to them, go to Bosque Redondo, or we will pursue and destroy you. We will not make peace with you on any other terms ... This war shall be pursued until you cease to exist or move. There can be no other talk on the subject."

The army was getting frustrated because they were finding very few Navajo. The Navajo were in hiding, but they were starving. The scorched earth policy was working.

Surrender and Long Walk

One thousand four hundred forty-three Navajos walked east from Fort Fauntleroy driving 473 horses and 3,000 sheep, to surrender. On their journey there, 10 people died and three children were kidnapped. When they arrived, they were given flour to eat. Not knowing what to do with it, they made a gruel like they would with corn mush. Eating this gave them serious diarrhea. When the group, which had grown to 2,400 people, was ready to leave a week later, those that were weak from diarrhea and dehydration were either shot or just left to die, especially if they were elderly.

Carleton had sent an order to the officers under his command saying,

> You will have corn or wheat issued to Indians if practicable at the rate of one pound a day to each ... the Indians will have no other food given to them except salt. In case meat is given to them, at times, it will be in lieu of the wheat or corn and at the same rate, i.e. one pound for each Indian, big and little." Upon receipt of this memo, Carson replied to Carleton saying, "I think one pound of beef, or of flour, wheat, or corn, is entirely too small an allowance for an able-bodied Indian for one day.

Captain Berney was in command of a group on the march to Bosque Redondo and on April 7, 1864, he made a report to headquarters writing,

> During the march the Indians suffered intensely from want of clothing, four were entirely frozen to death.
>
> On the 26th of February, the Indians having all arrived and transportation being in readiness, I had them moved about three miles from the post, and there put into lines, under the supervision of their chiefs, to have them counted. There proved to be in all fourteen hundred and forty-five (1445) Indians, having in their possession about two hundred horses and between three and four hundred sheep and goats. The Indians received a tolerable good supply of blankets and [sic] calicoes at Los Pinos. I took subsistence for fifteen days, at the rate of one pound of flour and one

pound of fresh beef per day, for each Indian, and a small portion of coffee and sugar for the chiefs.

On May 12, 1864, Captain McCabe reported on the group he was in command of writing,

> I placed as many of the women, children and old people as possible in wagons and had one empty wagon placed every morning under control of the Officer of the day for the purpose of traveling with the Guard to receive such sick and aged Indians as might have given out on the march.
>
> On the second day's march a very severe snow storm set in which lasted for four days with unusual severity and occasioned great suffering amongst the Indians, many of whom were nearly naked and of course unable to withstand such a storm. As I had barely a sufficient supply of rations and forage to enable me to reach Fort Wingate in the usual time, I could not encamp until the subsidence of the storm; although I desired very much to do so.

Grandma told us that as they walked, people were collapsing, many from starvation. If they couldn't walk, they were shot. It is likely my great-grandparents were part of this walk. No wonder Grandma warned us often to be careful about trusting white men.

The food they were furnished, while usually scant, often made them sick and several hundred died of food poisoning. The soldiers tried to get them to cover 15 miles each day, but often they could only manage 10. Sometimes, walkers had time to bury their dead relatives in a shallow grave before they started marching in the morning, but most of the time they had to just leave them at the mercy of the wild animals and birds.

They had been walking for nearly two and a half months but General Carleton, who was now directing the operation from Santa Fe, ordered the march to come through Albuquerque, Santa Fe and Fort Union, which added at least two additional weeks and 500 miles to the march. More than one hundred Navajo died between Albuquerque and Santa Fe. But Carleton wanted to show the public that the military had brought the fierce Navajo menace to an end under his command. The march through Santa Fe was publicized and the streets were lined with jeering, yelling people as the Navajo were marched through.

Just before they reached the Bosque Redondo reservation, the children who were marching contracted cholera and several died. Grandma said the walk killed many of the tribe, especially children and elderly.

Bosque Redondo

When they finally reached what had been promised as a wonderful paradise, they instead found a bare expanse of desert with a few cottonwood trees along the Pecos River. The water from the Pecos River made them sick, and there was no other source of water.

On arriving at Bosque Redondo, Lieutenant George Pettis wrote, "My dear wife, this is a terrible place … the Rio Pecos is a little stream winding through an immense plain, and the water is terrible, and it is all that can be had within 50 miles; it is full of alkali and operates on a person like castor oil, — take the water, heat it a little, and the more you wash yourself with common soap, the dirtier you get …."

Each Navajo family was assigned a plot of land to farm. While starving, they set about providing shelter for themselves and their families. There were obviously no logs to build hogans, so they dug holes in the ground with the shovels and picks they were furnished, and then covered the holes with branches. At least that was a little shelter from the elements. But how were they to keep warm and cook food when there was very little firewood to be had. The few cottonwood trees growing in the area were soon gone. Even the roots were dug up for firewood. Soon they were traveling 10-20 miles away from Fort Sumner in search of firewood.

When spring arrived, they prepared fields for planting and dug irrigation ditches for water from the Pecos. Long before harvest time came around, it became obvious the soil around Fort Sumner was poor in comparison to what they were used to in Navajo country. The pH of the soil was so alkaline that crops withered and died. That was only one of the problems their crops faced. With the lack of water and pests like cutworms, army worms and grasshoppers, their entire crop was a failure.

For three years they planted crops, including pumpkins, beans, wheat and corn, and for three years there was no harvest. Finally, they refused to plant. Grandma said the worst part was that they were starving. As children cried, then became quiet, and then died, they resorted to desperate measures, such as searching through the horse manure in the corral where they would find kernels of undigested corn that could be cleaned and cooked. The army issued them rations, but not nearly enough to stave off hunger, and people continued to starve every day.

In a moment of conscience, General Carleton wrote, "The Navajo are now proteges of the United States — a people who, having given up their country, should be provided for by a powerful and Christian nation." While Carleton had been ruthless in ordering the officers under his command to subdue the Navajo people and get them to Bosque Redondo, they were now there and Carleton was trying to get the supplies from the government needed to tide them over until they could become self-sufficient. When he asked for more food from Washington, he was told there is a Civil War going on and the Navajos can wait.

On March 5, 1864, Carleton sent a requisition for the needed supplies, but by September 16th they had still received nothing. Again, he wrote,

> As you are doubtless aware, I have now nearly eight thousand Indians upon the reservation at Bosque Redondo, who are almost entirely destitute of clothing and blanket, and now the cold weather is rapidly approaching. It is of vital importance that the articles which were to be purchased for the Indians with the hundred thousand dollars appropriated by Congress in its last session for this purpose, arrive at the Bosque Redondo and be distributed at the earliest practicable moment. … Let me impress upon your mind that unless they come, hundreds of naked women and children will be likely to perish…

By October 30th the supplies still had not been received. To add to this disaster, army worms had destroyed the Indian's crops, so they literally had nothing. Carleton again appealed, saying,

> … it is absolutely necessary that two thousand five hundred head of good cattle be bought in Kansas or Missouri, and sent out at once. … Then, if we cannot get bread, we can give the Indians more meat, and at least keep them from perishing.…"

The Navajo people were at the mercy of the government. The reservation food was kept locked up, and tickets were issued to each family to redeem for their share of food. They were allowed to hunt off the reservation, but they were forbidden to have firearms. Their only tools were bows and arrows and picks and shovels. In an effort to keep their families from starving, many of the women started trading sex with the soldiers for food. They must have been tormented when they thought about the creation story and how the spirit people were not welcome in the first worlds because of their adultery. Soon syphilis and other venereal diseases became common.

While Bosque Redondo was far enough away from the Utes and that threat disappeared, the Navajo were now closer to the Comanches who also snatched young women and girls and killed livestock.

Bosque Redondo reservation was a long way from Washington and got little attention, especially during the Civil War. But on January 29, 1865, even before the Civil War ended, a joint resolution was introduced in the Senate and was adopted on March 3rd to appoint a committee to investigate the condition of the Indian tribes and their treatment by the civil and military authorities. In 1865, Senator Doolittle of Wisconsin, who was chairman of the Committee on Indian Affairs, in his capacity as chairman of the Joint Special Committee on Conditions of Indian Tribes, visited Bosque Redondo and took his findings back to Washington. Even so, it took three more years for the United States government to realize that the army was starving the Navajo to death. Theodore Dodd was appointed agent to the Navajo tribe.

Ganado Mucho had escaped going to Bosque Redondo by leading his band into the Grand Canyon, but by the fall of 1865, he had decided to surrender. He probably questioned that decision as he made his way to Fort Sumner, because enroute his two youngest daughters were kidnapped by New Mexicans. After he reached his destination and reunited with his son, Ganado Blanco, his youngest son was killed by the Comanches.

When Superintendent of Indian Affairs, A.B. Norton, arrived to inspect Bosque Redondo, he met with Ganado Mucho, who pleaded with him to let his people return to their homeland. Ganado Mucho is quoted as saying to Norton, "I feel very bad. How can we protect ourselves when our enemies are much better armed than we are? We want to go back to our own country ... we want to go back there the same as we are here. The land here will never be as good as our own country. The government does not supply us with wood here, and we have plenty there. If the government would put us on a reservation in our own country and keep us the same as here within boundaries, the government would see how we work. We think we were born to live in our old country ... we think we are not born to live here."

In June of 1865, a group of Navajo, apparently including Barboncito and Manuelito, made an escape from Bosque Redondo and made their way toward home. A major effort was made by the military to recapture and return them or destroy them.

A little over a week later, Ganado Mucho's brother arrived at Bosque Redondo with news that Manuelito was still hiding but was wounded and weak. In September, Manuelito and 23 of his followers surrendered at Fort Wingate, and Manuelito was put in shackles. Barboncito was never caught, but eighteen months later, on November 7, 1866, he surrendered.

Twelve days after Manuelito surrendered, General Carleton was reassigned to Louisiana and Superintendent Norton called Ganado Mucho and nine other leaders to Santa Fe. He told them that Ulysses S. Grant had transferred their fate from the military to the civilian Indian Department.

Continuing his investigation, Senator Doolittle visited New Mexico Territory to study United States policy on Indians. When he interviewed Kit Carson, he asked why the New Mexicans were so opposed to the Navajos being left at Bosque Redondo. Carson reportedly replied that the slave market had dried up because there were no more Navajos to hunt.

In April of 1868, a delegation of Navajo leaders led by Indian Agent Theodore Dodd went to Santa Fe to ask Brigadier General George W. Getty to allow them to return to their homes. Getty deferred action until the leaders could meet with the newly established Peace Commission led by General William T. Sherman and Samuel F. Tappan. The Peace Commission arrived at Fort Sumner on May 27, 1868, and met in council with about 30 Navajo headmen.

The army was obviously getting tired of Bosque Redondo, and the Navajo did not want to be what the army wanted them to be. In the spring of 1868, they refused to plant crops since they never got a harvest from them anyway. Back in Washington in January of 1867, authority over the Navajo was moved from the army to the Bureau of Indian Affairs. That same week Kit Carson died of an aneurysm.

Photo Gallery

Me, (Verna) and my truck.

Me (Verna) in Cornfields. Do I look more Navajo with my hair dyed black?

Me (Verna) making breakfast when we lived in Parker, AZ.

Me (Verna) at Lake Havasu City.

Me (Verna) watching construction on Hoover Dam.

Me (Verna) at Cornfields, AZ.

Me (Verna).

Me (Verna).

Brother Ray, me (Verna) and brother Lynn.

Sister Marilyn, left, and me (Verna).

My (Verna's) brothers, left to right: Martinez, Alfred, Kenneth, Gilbert and Nelson.

Left to right, Uncle Joe, Me (Verna) and brother Lynn.

Left to right, Uncle Joe, brother Lynn and Uncle Ellis.

My (Verna's) sister Geneva and her son Jeremiah.

My (Verna's) brother Alfred.

Me (Verna) with sister Marilyn.

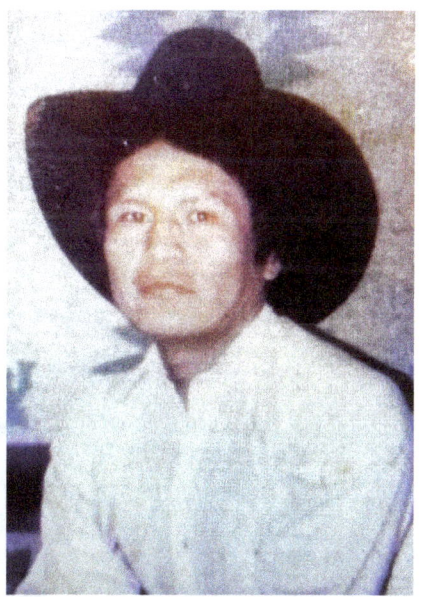

My (Verna's) oldest brother Wilbert (Willie).

My (Verna's) brothers, left to right, Nelson, Martinez and Kenneth.

Left to right, daughter Harranna, son Harry, and daughter Veranna.

Daughters, back row, left to right: Angela and Vernadine Front row: left to right, Denise and Veronica.

Below, left to right, grandson Juan, daughter Manda, granddaughters Vanessa and Gabriella and daughter Mandy.

Above, left to right, daughters Angela and Harranna, me (Verna), daughter Vernadine and son Harry.

Camp Pendleton Marine base. Back row, left to right, daughters Vernadine, Angela, Veronica, Denise and Harranna. Front row, left to right, son Harry, and daughters Veranna, Mandy and Manda.

My (Verna's) daughter Angela graduating from preschool.

Daughters Denise, left, and Veronica, right, at preschool graduation.

My kiddies in Parker, AZ, from left to right: Vernadine holding Harry, Veronica, Harranna, Denise and Angela.

Left to right: me (Verna), daughter Manda and granddaughter Gabriella.

Left to right: My (Verna's) son Harry, daughters Veranna and Harranna, with sister Geneva behind them.

Left to right: daughter Mandy, me (Verna), and daughter Veronica.

*Son Harry hunt-
ing Easter eggs at
Steamboat, AZ.*

Daughter Veranna and son Harry.

Son Harry.

Daughter Denise and son Harry.

Back row, left to right, daughter Angela, son-in-law Gilbert, daughter Harranna. Middle row, left to right: husband Manley, me (Verna), daughter Denise and daughter Veranna. Front row, left to right: daughters Manda and Mandy and granddaughter Gabriella.

Left to right, daughters Harranna, Veronica, Veranna, Denise, Vernadine, Angela, me (Verna) and husband Manley.

Manley, holding Manda, Me (Verna), and Veronica.

From left to right, Manda, Me (Verna) and Manley
at Manda's 16th birthday.

Gabriella's wedding. Back row, left to right: Manda, Vernadine, Angela, Mandy, Veronica, Denise, Veranna, Harranna, and Harry. Front seated, left to right: Shawn, Gabriella.

Back row from left to right: Manda, Angela, Veronica, Denise, Harranna, Harry. Front Row from left to right: Vernadine, Mandy, Veranna, Me (Verna), Manley.

Back row, left to right, Daughter Mandy, borther Lynn, daughters Angela and Harranna. Front row, left to right: granddaughter Gabriella, me (Verna) and daughter Manda.

Daughter Manda and Marcus with baby Marcus Jr.

Daughters Harranna, left and Angela, right.

Daughter Angela, front, me (Verna) on left; Manley, seated center; and sister Marilyn, right.

My (Verna's) daughter Harranna and grandson Alex.

Son Harry with Angelina on his left, with my (Verna's) granddaughters Rosalinda, left and Makayla, right.

My family in Tijuana, Mexico. Left to right, son Harry, daughters Denise and Manda, me (Verna), daughters Mandy, Veranna, Harranna, and Veronica.

*Son-in-law Kris and daughter
Harranna.*

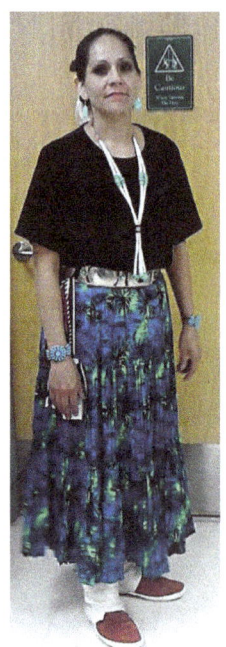

*Daughter
Harranna in
traditional dress.*

Manley and daughter Manda.

Me (Verna) with grandson Marcus.

Grandsons Tobias, left, and Kristo in the truck helping grandma haul Blue Bird flour.

Left to right, grandson Samuel, granddaughter Alicia and grandson Marcus.

Grandson Marcus helping grandma buy Blue Bird flour.

Grandson Marcus and daughter Manda.

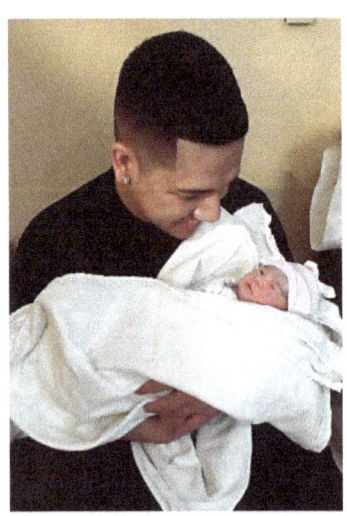

Grandson Christopher holding great grandbaby.

Me (Verna) holding grandson Samuel.

*Me (Verna) with most of my grandchildren and holding a great grandchild.
Now do you understand why I have trouble remembering all their names?*

*Four generations. Left to right, me (Verna), great granddaughter Evelyn,
daughter Vernadine and granddaughter Vanessa.*

*Granddaughter Malia
enjoying chili beans in
the traditional way.*

*Granddaughter Alisa
about to enjoy a
frybread.*

From left to right: Grandson Juan, daughter Vernadine, granddaughters Lily and Alisa, grandson Anthony, granddaughter Vanessa and grandson Christopher.

Back row, son-in-law Brandon and daughter Denise. Front row, from left to right, granddaughters Malia and Jesse.

Left to right, my (Verna's) grandson Samuel, daughter Mandy and granddaughter Alicia.

Left to right, my (Verna's) daughter Mandy with grandson graduate Samuel and granddaughter Alicia.

Family outing at Phoenix Zoo.

From left to right: grandsons Alex, Noel, Kristo, daughter Harranna, and grandson Tobias.

Grandchildren Juan, Gabriella and Christopher.

Grandchildren Alicia and Samuel —
future code talkers?

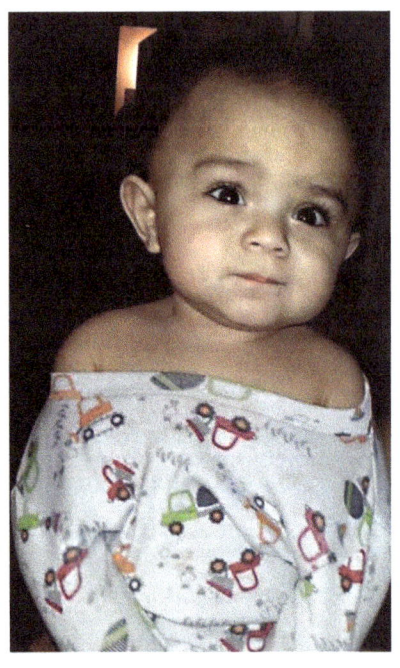

Alicia and Marcus after Marcus won his match.

Grandson Marcus in detention.

Grandson Samuels's high school graduation. Left to right: Manley, Me (Verna), Samuel, Alicia and Marcus.

Proud Marcus at his promotion.

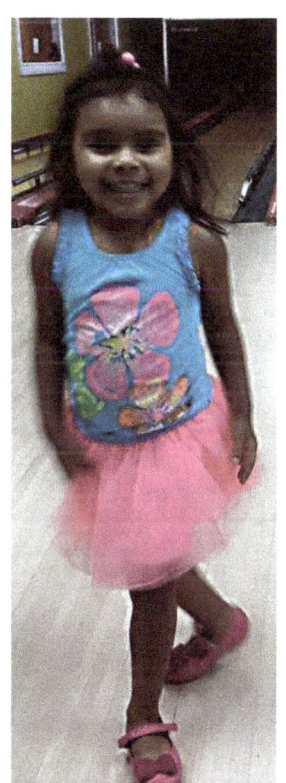

Granddaughter Laila at the bowling alley.

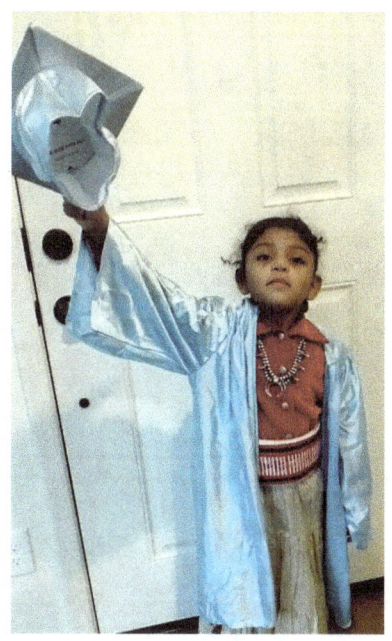

Granddaughter Jesse at her graduation.

Granddaughters Malia and Jesse.

143

Granddaughter Esperanza (Ava).

Granddaughter Laila.

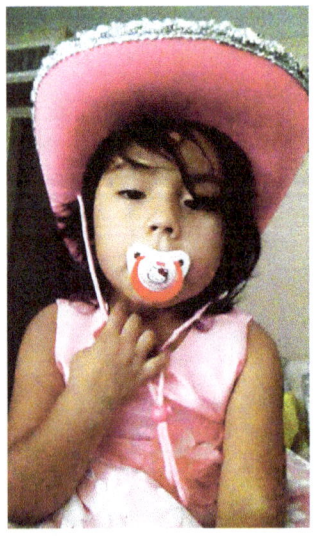

Granddaughter Esperanza (Ava).

Granddaughter Vanessa and great granddaughter Evelyn.

Grandson Noel and daughter Harranna.

Granddaughter Lily and grandson Marcus.

Grandson Marcus (with glasses), Manda and Jupiter.

Left to right: grandchildren Romeo, holding Isaih, Destiny holding Annalisa, Amiya, Eddie.

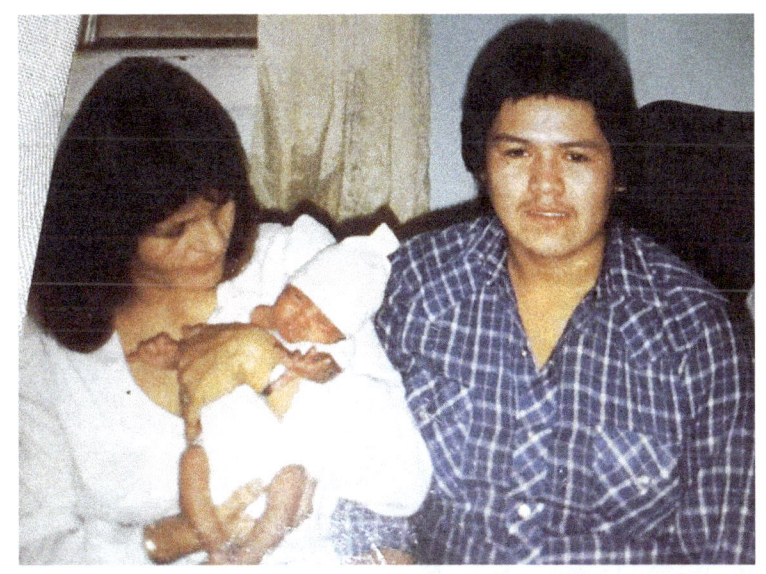

Me (Verna) and Manley with baby Mandy.

Me (Verna) and grandson Marcus.

Me (Verna) with my common-law husband Manley who helped me raise my (our) 9 children.

My (Verna's) grandsons acting tough. Left to right: Romeo, Samuel, Merced and Mateo.

Left to right: grandsons Alex, Tobias, Noel, daughter Harranna, son-in-law Kris, and grandson Kristo.

My (Verna's) grandchildren. From left to right, front row: Samuel, Alicia, Amyia. Back row: Romeo, Destiny.

My (Verna's) granddaughter Laila.

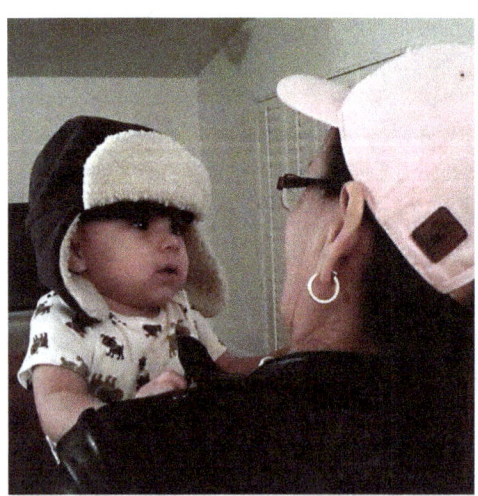

Daughter Veronica, granddaughter Laila, and son-in-law Lorenzo.

Grandma Verna singing to grandson Marcus.

Daughter Manda and grandson Marcus.

My (Verna's) granddaughter Vanessa.

*My (Verna's) granddaughters
Malia, left, and Jesse, right.*

*My (Verna's) grandson
Merced.*

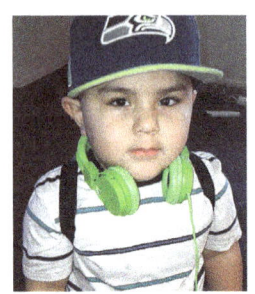

My grandson Marcus, a Seahawks fan.

Shawn and Gabriella.

Grand son-in-law Spencer and grand-daughter Alisa.

Left to right: Grandsons Mateo and Merced.

Grandson Samuel and granddaughter Alicia.

Grandson Mateo, granddaughter Esperanza (Ava) and grandson Merced.

Granddaughter Gabriella.

Grandson Marcus.

Manley and grandson Samuel.

Granddaughter Alicia, a runner.

Left to right: granddaughter Gabriella, me (Verna) holding grandson Romeo, granddaughters Vanessa and Alisa and grandsons Juan and Christopher.

Me (Verna), left, and sister Marilyn.

Me (Verna) about 1996.

Me (Verna) at home.

*Me (Verna) the lady in
pink.*

Me (Verna) deciding which horse to ride.

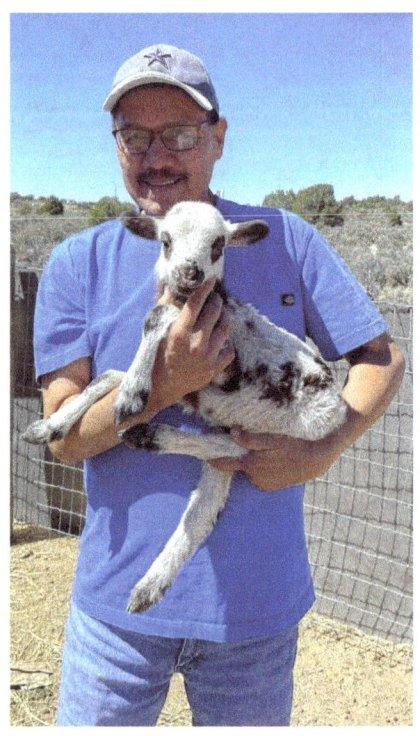

Manley carying a lamb.

Me (Verna) with my friend Maizie.

Manley at home on the Rez feeding the sheep.

Manley and Jupiter.

Manley and Me (Verna).

Long delayed brother-sister love.
Me (Verna) and brother Lynn.

Me (Verna) and Grandma Stella.

Back row, Left to right: daughter Angela, Uncle Joe, brother Lynn and daughter Mandy. Front row, left to right: daughter Manda, me (Verna), and granddaughter Gabriella.

Me (Verna) and brother Lynn.

Left to right: Uncle Joe, me (Verna) and brother Lynn.

Left to right: Uncle Ellis, Me (Verna) and daughter Angela.

*Brother Lynn and Grandma Stella
at Uncle Ellis's festival.*

*Grandpa Ruel Leji Tanner and Grandma
Stella McGee Tanner.*

My (Verna's) great-great-grandpa was Seth Benjamin Tanner (1828–1918) and my great-great-grandma was Charlotte Levi Tanner (pictured above). Their son, John Tanner (1860–1947), was my great-grandpa, and Elizabeth Beswick Tanner was my great-grandma.

Me (Verna) and Uncle Joe working on our family tree..

CHAPTER 13

The Peace Commission

T he Navajo people were prisoners in a place where life as they knew it was impossible. This place was not what the government had promised them, and finally the Government knew it.

On May 28, 1868, a council met with General William Tecumseh Sherman and Samuel F. Tappan representing the United States, and the Chiefs and Headmen representing the Navajo tribe. The chiefs present were Delgadito, Barboncito, Manuelito, Largo, Herrero, Armijo, and Torivio. Jesus Alviso was the Indian interpreter and James Sutherland was the Spanish interpreter.

General Sherman opened the council, saying, "The Commissioners are here now for the purpose of learning and knowing all about your condition and we wish to hear from you the truth and nothing but the truth. We have read in our books and learned from our officers that for many years whether right or wrong the Navajos have been at war with us and that General Carleton had removed you here for the purpose of making you agriculturists — with that view the Government of the United States gave you money and built this fort to protect you until you were able to protect yourselves. We find you have done a good deal of work here in making acequias [irrigation system], but we find you have no farms, no herds and are now as poor as you were four years ago. That before we discuss what we are to do with you, we want to know what you have done in the past and what you think about your reservation here."

Barboncito

Barboncito replied,

The bringing of us here has caused a great decrease of our numbers, many of us have died, also a great number of our animals. Our Grandfathers had no idea of living in any other country except our own and I do not think it right for us to do so as we were never taught to. When the Navajos were first created four mountains and four rivers were pointed out to us, inside of which we should live, that was to be our country and was given to us by the first woman of the Navajo tribe. It was told to us by our forefathers, that we were never to move east of the Rio Grande or west of the San Juan rivers and I think that our coming here has been the cause of so much death among us and our animals.

That our God when he was created (the woman I spoke of) gave us this piece of land and created it specially for us and gave us the whitest of corn and the best of horses and sheep. You can see them (pointing to the other chiefs) ordinarily looking as they are. I think that when the last of them is gone the world will come to an end. — It is true we were brought here; also true we have been taken good care of since we have been here. — As soon as we were brought here, we started into work making acequias (and I myself went to work with my party) we made all the adobes you see here, we have always done as we were told to, if told to bring ashes from the hearth we would do so, carry water and herd stock, we never refused to do anything we were told to do.

This ground we were brought on, it is not productive, we plant but it does not yield, all the stock we brought here have nearly all died. Because we were brought here we have done all we could possibly do, but found it to be labor in vain, and have therefore quit it, for that reason we have not planted or tried to do anything this year. It is true we put seed in the ground but it would not grow two feet high, the reason I cannot tell, only I think this ground was never intended for us, we know how to irrigate and farm, still we cannot raise a crop here, we know how to plant all kinds of seed, and how to raise stock, and take care of it.

The Commissioners can see themselves that we have barely any sheep or horses, nearly all that we brought here have died and that has left us so poor that we have no means wherewith to buy others. — There are a great many among us who were once well off, now they have nothing in their houses to sleep on except gunny sacks. True some of us have a little stock left yet, but not near what we had some years ago, in our old country. For that reason, my mouth is dry and my head hangs in sorrow to see those around me who were at one time well off so poor now.

When we had a way of living of our own, we lived happy, we had plenty of stock, nothing to do but look at our stock, and when we wanted meat nothing to do but kill it. They were once rich (pointing to the chiefs present). I feel sorry at the way I am fixed here, I cannot rest comfortable at night, I am ashamed to go to the commissary for my food, it looks as if somebody was waiting to give it to me.

Since the time I was very small until I was a man, when I had my father and mother to take care of, I had plenty, and since that time I have always followed my father's advice and still keep it. Viz: [that is to say] to live at peace with everybody.

I want to tell the Commissioners I was born at the lower end of Canon de Chelly. We have been living here five winters. The first year we planted corn, it yielded a good crop but a worm got in the corn and destroyed nearly all of it. The second year the same; the third year it grew about two feet high then a hail storm completely destroyed all of it. We have done all we possibly could to raise a crop of corn and pumpkins but we were disappointed.

I thought at one time the whole world was the same as my own country but I got fooled. Outside my own country, we cannot raise a crop, but in it we can raise a crop almost anywhere. Our families and stock increase there, here they decrease. We know this land does not like us; neither does the water. They have all said this ground was not intended for us, for that reason none of us have attempted to put in seed this year.

I think now it is true what my forefathers told me about crossing the line of my own country. It seems that whatever we do here causes death. Some work at the Acequias take sick and die, others die with the hoe in their hands, they go to the river to their waists and suddenly disappear. Others have been struck and torn to pieces by lightning. A rattle-snake bite here kills us; in our own country a rattlesnake before he bites gives warning which enables us to keep out of its way and if bitten, we readily find a cure; here we find no cure.

When one of our big men die, the cries of the women causes tears to roll down onto my moustache. I then think of my own country. I think the Commissioners have seen one thing, when we came here there was plenty of mesquite root that we used for fuel, now there is none nearer than the place where I met the Commissioners, 25 miles from here. In the winter, many die from cold and sickness and overworking from carrying wood such a long distance on their backs. For that reason, we cannot stay contented where we now are.

Some years ago, I could raise my head and see herds of cattle in any direction. Now, I feel sorry I cannot see any. I raise my head and can see herds of stock on my right and left, but they are not mine. It makes me feel sorry thinking of the time when I had plenty. I can scarcely endure it. I think that all nations 'round here are against us (I mean Mexicans and Indians). The reason is that we are a working tribe of Indians, and if we had the means, we could support ourselves far better than either Mexican or Indian.

The Comanches are against us, I know it, for they came here and killed a good many of our men. In our own country we knew nothing about the Comanches. Last winter, I heard said that there was a Commission coming here now. I am happy it has arrived, for I expect to hear from the Commission today the object of its coming here.

We have all declared that we do not want to remain here any longer. If I can complete my thoughts today, I will give the General my best thanks and think of him as my father and mother. As soon as I heard of your coming, I made three pair of moccasins and have worn out two pair of them since. As you see yourselves, I am strong and hearty and before I am sick or older I want to go and see the place where I was born. Now I am just like a woman, sorry like a woman in trouble. I want to go and see my own country.

If we are taken back to our own country, we will call you our father and mother. If you should only tie a goat there we would all live off it, all of the same opinion. I am speaking for the whole tribe, for their animals from the horse to the dog, also the unborn. All that you have heard now is the truth and is the opinion of the whole tribe. It appears to me that the General commands the whole thing as a god. I hope therefore, he will do all he can for the Indian. This hope goes in at my feet and out at my mouth. I am speaking to you [General Sherman] now as if I was speaking to a spirit and I wish you to tell me when you are going to take us to our own country.

Following the introductory speeches by Sherman and Barboncito, Sherman tried to generate some interest in moving them to the Indian Country where the five civilized tribes had been moved. He suggested that a delegation of Navajo be sent there to see for themselves. He also emphasized that if they were moved, they must not use revenge as a way of settling disagreements but must let the government soldiers do the fighting. He explained that if they were returned to their old country, there would be strict boundaries across which they could go only for trade.

Barboncito replied, "I hope to God you will not ask me to go to any other country except my own. It might turn out another Bosque Redondo. They told us this was a good place when we came, but it is not."

Sherman could see that it was useless to talk about moving them anywhere but to their old country, so he scheduled another council for the next day. He asked them to select a committee of 10 men to work with the Commissioners on establishing boundary lines in their own country.

Again, Barboncito responded, "I am very well pleased with what you have said, and if we go back to our own country, we are willing to abide by whatever orders are issued to us. We do not want to go to the right or left, but straight back to our own country."

The next day, General Sherman chaired the council and explained to the whole tribe that the Commission was giving them three choices:

(1) any Navajo could go wherever he pleased in this territory and settle with his family, but if he did this he would be subject to the laws of the Territory as a citizen,

(2) they could choose, as a tribe, to be removed to Indian Country (Cherokee Country) or

(3) they could be moved, as a tribe, back to their own country." Sherman reported, "Yesterday Barboncito insisted strongly on going back to his own country in preference to the other two propositions.

Ten men had been selected to work with the commissioners on the terms of a treaty: Delgadito, Barboncito, Manuelito, Largo, Herrero, Chiqueto, Murerto de Hombre, Hombro, Narbono and Armijo, with Barboncito as the Chief. After these actions were approved unanimously by a yes vote, Sherman proceeded to speak to the tribe as if they were children saying,

> From this time out you must do as Barboncito tells you. With him we will deal and do all for your good. When you leave here and go to your own country you must do as he tells you and when you get to your country you must obey him or he will punish you. If he has not the power to do so he will call on the soldiers and they will do it. You must all keep together on the march. You must not scatter for I fear some of your young men might do wrong and get you all into trouble.

To this point in the conversations they had talked about boundary lines, but then Barboncito must have remembered a conversation he had the day before. He spoke up saying, "You spoke to me yesterday about putting us on a reservation with a boundary line. I do not think it is right to confine us to a certain part; we want to have the privilege of going outside the line to hunt and trade."

Sherman replied, "You can go outside the line to hunt — you can go to Mexican towns to trade — but your farms and homes must be inside the boundary line, because beyond it you have no claim to the land."

Barboncito said, "That is the way I like to be and return the Commissioners my best thanks." He went on to talk about how great life would be when they got back to their own country and then said, "I want to drop this conversation now and talk about Navajo children held as prisoners by Mexicans. Some of those present have lost a brother or a sister and I know that they are in the hands of the Mexicans. I have seen some myself."

General Sherman's reply was, "About their children being held as peons by Mexicans — you ought to know that there is an Act of Congress against it. About four years ago we had slaves and there was a great war about it, now there are none. Congress, our great council, passed a law prohibiting peonage in New Mexico. So if any Mexican holds a Navajo in peonage he (the Mexican) is liable to be put in the penitentiary. We do not know that there are any Navajos held by Mexicans as peons but if there are, you can apply to the judges of the civil courts and the land commissioners. They are the proper persons to handle this and they will decide whether the Navajo is to go back to his own people or remain with the Mexican. That is a matter with which we have nothing to do." With that he changed the subject back to the treaty.

Colonel Tappan, who it is interesting to note was an abolitionist who had grown up in Massachusetts, brought the conversation back to the slavery issue. He asked, "How many Navajos are among the Mexicans now?"

Someone answered, "Over half the tribe."

General Sherman then returned to the issue saying,

> We will do all we can to have your children returned to you. Our government is determined that the enslavement of the Navajos shall cease and those who are guilty of holding them as peons shall be punished. All are now free to come and go as they please in this country. If children are held in peonage, the courts will decide. You can go where any Navajos are and General Getty will give you an order or send a soldier. If the Navajo peons wish to come back or remain, he can please himself. We will not use force; the courts must decide.

(In Chapter 11 we discussed our opinion that the Navajo slavery issue was probably the major cause of the Navajo wars. Here we see that the only thing the Navajos asked for from the Peace Commission, besides being allowed to go back to their own country, was help with the slavery issue. Perhaps this is more evidence that we are right.)

The following day, the proposed treaty was read to the 10 chiefs (headmen) and they approved it. General Sherman then said, "We have marked off a reservation for you, including the Canon de Chelly and part of the valley of the San Juan. It is about 100 square miles. It runs as far south as Canon Bonito and includes the Chusca Mountain but not the Mesa Calabesa you spoke of; that is the reservation we suggest to you. It also includes the Ceresca Mountain and the bend of the San Juan river, not the upper waters."

Barboncito replied, "We are very well pleased with what you have said and well satisfied with that reservation. It is the very heart of our country and is more than we ever expected to get." He then asked that Narbono Segundo and Ganado Mucho be added to the Council of Ten and it was agreed to.

Ganado Mucho then said, "After what the Commissioners have said, I do not think anybody has anything to say. After we go back to our own country it will be the same as it used to be. We have never found any person heretofore who told us what you now have and when we return to our own country we will return you our best thanks. We understand the good news you have told us to be right, and we like it very much; we have been

Ganado Mucho

waiting for a long time to hear the good words you have now told us about going back to our own country. I will not stop talking until I have told all the tribe the good news."

The treaty was signed on June 1, 1868. Ganado Mucho had said it well. The Navajo tribe was happy.

The Navajo Treaty—1868

ANDREW JOHNSON
PRESIDENT OF THE UNITED STATES OF AMERICA

TO ALL AND SINGULAR TO WHOM PRESIDENTS
SHALL COME GREETING:

Whereas a treaty was made and concluded at Fort Sumner in the Territory of New Mexico on the first day of June, in the year of our Lord one thousand eight hundred and sixty-eight, by and between Lieutenant General W.T Sherman and Samuel F. Tappan, Commissioners, on the part of the United States, and Barboncito, Armijo and other Chiefs and Headmen of the Navajo tribe of Indians, on the part of said Indians, and duly authorized by them, which Treaty is in words and figures following, to wit:

Articles of a Treaty and Agreement made and entered into at Fort Sumner, New Mexico, on the first day of June , 1868, by and between the United States, represented by its Commissioners, Lieutenant General W.T. Sherman and Colonel Samuel F. Tappan, of the one part, and the Navajo nation or tribe of Indians, represented by their Chiefs and Headmen, duly authorized and empowered to act for the whole people of said nation or tribe, (the names of said Chiefs and Headmen being hereto subscribed,) of the other part, witness:

ARTICLE I

From this day forward all war between the parties to this agreement shall for ever cease. The government of the United States desires peace, and its honor is hereby pledged to keep it. The Indians desire peace, and they now pledge their honor to keep it.

If bad men among the whites, or among other people subject to the authority of the United States, shall commit any wrong upon the person or property of the Indians, the United States will, upon proof made to the agent and forwarded to the Commissioner of Indian Affairs at Washington city, proceed at once to cause the offender to be arrested and punished according to the laws of the United States, and also to reimburse the injured person for the loss sustained.

If bad men among the Indians shall commit a wrong or depredation upon the person or property of anyone, white, black, or Indian, subject to the authority of the United States and at peace therewith, the Navajo tribe agree that they will, on proof made to their agent, and on notice by him, deliver up the wrongdoer to the United States, to be tried and punished according to the laws; and in case they willfully refuse so to do, the person injured shall be reimbursed for his loss from the annuities or other moneys due or to become due them under this treaty, or any others that may be made with the United States. And the President may prescribe such rules and regulations for ascertaining damages under this article as in his judgment may be proper; but no such damage shall be adjusted and paid until examined and passed upon by the Commissioner of Indian Affairs, and no one sustaining loss whilst violating, or because of his violating, the provision of this treaty or the laws of the United States shall be reimbursed therefor.

ARTICLE II

The United States agrees that the following district of country, to wit: bounded on the north by the 37th degree of north latitude, south by an east and west line passing through the site of old Fort Defiance, in Canon Bonito, east by the parallel of longitude which, if prolonged south, would pass through old Fort Lyon, or the Ojo-de-oso, Bear Spring, and west by a parallel of longitude about 109° 30' west of Greenwich, provided it embraces the outlet of the Canon de Chelly, which canon is to be all included in this reservation, shall be, and the same is hereby, set apart for the use and occupation of the Navajo tribe of Indians, and for such other friendly tribes or individual Indians as from time to time they may be willing, with the consent of the United States, to admit among them; and the United States agrees that no persons except those herein so authorized to do, and except such officers, soldiers, agents, and employees of the government , or of the Indians, as may be authorized to enter upon Indian reservations in discharge of duties imposed by law, or the orders of the President, shall ever be permitted to pass over, settle upon, or reside in, the territory described in this article.

ARTICLE III

The United States agrees to cause to be built at some point within said reservation, where timber and water may be convenient, the following buildings; a warehouse, to cost not exceeding twenty-five hundred dollars; an agency building for the residence of the agent, not to cost exceeding three thousand dollars; a carpenter shop and blacksmith shop, not to exceed one thousand dollars each; and a school house and chapel, so soon as a sufficient number of children can be induced to attend school, which shall not cost to exceed five thousand dollars

ARTICLE IV

The United States agrees that the agent for the Navajos shall make his home at the agency building; that he shall reside among them and shall keep an office open at all times for the purpose of prompt and diligent inquiry into such matters of complaint by or against the Indians as may be presented for investigation, as also for the faithful discharge of other duties enjoined by law. In all cases of depredation on person or property he shall cause the evidence to be taken in writing and forwarded, together with his finding, to the Commissioner of Indian Affairs, whose decision shall be binding on the parties to this treaty.

ARTICLE V

If any individual belonging to said tribe, or legally incorporated with it, being the head of a family, shall desire to commence farming, he shall have the privilege to select, in the presence and with the assistance of the agent then in charge, a tract of land within said reservation, not exceeding one hundred and sixty acres in extent, which tract when so selected, certified, and recorded in the "land book" as herein described shall cease to be held in common, but the same may be occupied and held in the exclusive possession of the person selecting it, and of his family, so long as he or they may continue to cultivate it.

Any person over eighteen years of age, not being the head of the family, may in like manner select, and cause to be certified to him or her for purposes of cultivation, a quantity of land, not exceeding eighty acres in extent, and thereupon be entitled to the exclusive possession of the same as above directed.

For each tract of land so selected a certificate containing a description thereof, and the name of the person selecting it, with a certificate endorsed thereon that the same has been recorded, shall be delivered to the party entitled to it by the agent, after the same shall have been recorded by him in a book to be kept in his office, subject to inspection which said book shall be known as the "Navajo Land Book."

The President may at any time order a survey of the reservation and, when so surveyed, Congress shall provide for protecting the rights of said settlers in their improvements, and may fix the character of the title held by each. The United States may pass such laws on the subject of alienation and descent of property between the Indians and their descendants as may be thought proper.

ARTICLE VI

In order to insure the civilization of the Indians entering into this treaty, the necessity of education is admitted, especially of such of them as may be settled on said agricultural parts of this reservation, and they therefore pledge themselves to compel their children, male and female, between the ages of six and sixteen years, to attend school; and it is hereby made the duty of the agent for said Indians to see that this stipulation is strictly complied with; and the United States agrees that, for every thirty children between said ages who can be induced or compelled to attend school, a house shall be provided, and a teacher competent to teach the elementary branches of an English education shall be furnished, who will reside among said Indians, and faithfully discharge his or her duties as a teacher.

The provisions of this article to continue for not less than ten years.

ARTICLE VII

When the head of a family shall have selected lands and received his certificate as above directed, and the agent shall be satisfied that he intends in good faith to commence cultivating the soil for a living, he shall be entitled to receive seeds and agricultural implements for the first year, not exceeding in value one hundred dollars, and for each succeeding year he shall continue to farm, for a period of two years, he shall be entitled to receive seeds and implements to the value of twenty-five dollars.

ARTICLE VIII

In lieu of all sums of money or other annuities provided to be paid for the Indians herein named under any treaty or treaties heretofore made, the United States agrees to deliver at the agency house on the reservation herein named, on the first day of September of each year for ten years, the following articles to wit:

Such articles of clothing, goods, or raw materials in lieu thereof, as the agent may make his estimate for, not exceeding in value five dollars per Indian – each Indian being encouraged to manufacture their own clothing, blankets, etc.; to be furnished with no article which they can manufacture themselves. And in order that the Commissioner of Indian Affairs may be able to estimate properly for the articles herein named, it shall be the duty of the agent each year to forward to him a full and exact census of the Indians on which the estimate from year to year can be based.

And in addition to the articles herein named, the sum of ten dollars for each person entitled to the beneficial effects of this treaty shall be annually appropriated for a period of ten years, for each person who engages in farming or mechanical pursuits, to be used by the Commissioner of Indian Affairs in the purchase of such articles as from time to time the condition and necessities of the Indian may indicate to be proper; and if within the ten years at anytime it shall appear that the amount of money needed for clothing, under the article, can be appropriated to better uses for the Indians named herein, the Commissioner of Indian Affairs may change the appropriation to other purposes, but in no event shall the amount of this appropriation be withdrawn or discontinued for the period named, provided they remain at peace. And the President shall annually detail an officer of the army to be present and attest the delivery of all the goods herein named to the Indians, and he shall inspect and report on the quantity and quality of the goods and the manner of their delivery.

ARTICLE IX

In consideration of the advantages and benefits conferred by this treaty, and the many pledges of friendship by the United States, the tribes who are parties to this agreement hereby stipulate that they will relinquish all right to occupy any territory outside their reservation, as herein defined, but retain the right to hunt on any unoccupied lands contiguous to their reservation, so long as the large game may range thereon in such numbers to justify the chase; and they, the said Indians, further expressly agree:

1st. That they will make no opposition to the construction of railroads now being built or hereafter to be built, across the continent.

2nd. That they will not interfere with the peaceful construction of any railroad not passing over their reservation as herein defined.

3rd. That they will not attack any persons at home or traveling, nor molest or disturb any wagon trains, coaches, mules or cattle belonging to the people of the United States or to persons friendly therewith.

4th. That they will never capture or carry off from the settlements women or children.

5th. They will never kill or scalp white men, nor attempt to do them harm.

6th. They will not in future oppose the construction of railroads, wagon roads, mail stations, or other works of utility or necessity which may be ordered or permitted by the laws of the United States; but should such roads or other works be constructed on the lands of their reservation, the government will pay the tribe whatever amount of damage may be assessed by three disinterested commissioners to be appointed by the President for that purpose, one of said commissioners to be a chief or head man of the tribe.

7th. They will make no opposition to the military posts or roads now established, or that may be established, not in violation of treaties heretofore made or hereafter to be made with any of the Indian tribes.

ARTICLE X

No future treaty for the cession of any portion or part of the reservation herein described, which may be held in common, shall be of any validity or force against said Indians unless agreed to and executed by at least three-fourths of all the adult male Indians occupying or interested in the same; and no cession by the tribe shall be understood or construed in such manner as to deprive, without his consent, any individual member of the tribe of his rights to any tract of land selected by him as provided in article 5 of this treaty.

ARTICLE XI

The Navajos also hereby agree that at any time after the signing of these presents they will proceed in such manner as may be required of them by the agent, or by the officer charged with their removal, to the reservation herein provided for, the United States paying for their subsistence en route, and providing a reasonable amount of transportation for the sick and feeble.

ARTICLE XII

It is further agreed by and between the parties to this agreement that the sum of one hundred and fifty thousand dollars appropriated or to be appropriated shall be disbursed as follows, subject to any conditions provided in the law, to wit:

1st. The actual cost of the removal of the tribe from the Bosque Redondo reservation to the reservation, say fifty thousand dollars.

2nd. The purchase of fifteen thousand sheep and goats, at a cost not to exceed thirty thousand dollars.

3rd. The purchase of five hundred beef cattle and a million pounds of corn, to be collected and held at the military post nearest the reservation, subject to the orders of the agent, for the relief of the needy during the coming winter.

4th. The balance, if any, of the appropriation to be invested for the maintenance of the Indians pending their removal, in such manner as the agent who is with them may determine.

5th. The removal of this tribe to be made under the supreme control and direction of the military commander of the Territory of New Mexico, and when completed, the management of the tribe to revert to the proper agent.

ARTICLE XIII

The tribe herein named, by their representatives, parties to this treaty, agree to make the reservation herein described their permanent home, and they will not as a tribe make any permanent settlement elsewhere, reserving the right to hunt on the lands adjoining the said reservation formerly called theirs, subject to the modifications named in this treaty and the orders of the commander of the department in which said reservation may be for the time being; and it is further agreed and understood by the parties to this treaty, that if any Navajo Indian or Indians shall leave the reservation herein described to settle elsewhere, he or they shall forfeit all the rights, privileges, and annuities conferred by the terms of this treaty; and it is further agreed by the parties to this treaty, that they will do all they can to induce Indians now away from the reservations set apart for the exclusive use and occupation of the Indians, leading a nomadic life, or engaged in war against the people of the United States to abandon such a life and settle permanently in one of the territorial reservations set apart for the exclusive use and occupation of the Indians.

In testimony of all which the said parties have hereunto, on this the first day of June, eighteen hundred and sixty-eight, at Fort Sumner, in the Territory of New Mexico, set their hands and seals.

W. T. SHERMAN
Lt. Gen'l Indian Peace Commissioner

S. F. TAPPAN
Indian Peace Commissioner

BARBONCITO, *Chief* (his x mark
ARMIJO (his x mark)
DELGADO (his x mark)
MANUELITO (his x mark)
LARGO (his x mark)
HERRERO (his x mark)
CHIQUETO (his x mark)
MUERTO DE HOMBRE (his x mark)
HOMBRO (his x mark)
NARBONO (his x mark)
NARBONO SEGUNDO (his x mark)
GANADO MUCHO (his x mark)

COUNCIL
RIQUO (his x mark)
JUAN MARTIN (his x mark)
SERGINTO (his x mark)
GRANDE (his x mark)
INOETENITO (his x mark)
MUCHACHOS MUCHO
   (his x mark)
CHIQUETO SEGUNDO
   (his x mark)
CABELLO AMARILLO (his x mark)
FRANCISCO (his x mark)
TORIVIO (his x mark)
DESDENDADO (his x mark)
JUAN (his x mark)
GUERO (his x mark)

GUGADORE (his x mark)
CABASON (his x mark)
BARBON SEGUNDO (his x mark)
CABARES COLORADOS
   (his x mark)

Attest:
Geo. W.G. Getty
Col. 37ᵗʰ Inf'y Bt. Maj. Gen'l U.S.A.
B.S. Roberts
Bt. Brg. Gen'l U.S.A. Lt. Col. 3ʳᵈ Cav'y
J. Cooper Mckee
Bt. Lt. Col. Surgeon U.S.A.
Theo. H. Dodd
U.S. Indian Ag't for Navajos
Chas. McClure
Bt. Maj. And C.S. U.S.A.
James F. Weeds
Bt. Maj. And Asst. Surg. U.S.A.
J.C. Sutherland
Interpreter
William Vaux
Chaplain U.S.A.

And whereas, the said treaty having been submitted to the Senate of the United States for its constitutional action thereon, the Senate did, on the twenty-fifth day of July, one thousand eight hundred and sixty-eight, advise and consent to the ratification of the same, by a resolution in the words and figures following to wit:

Resolved, (two-thirds of the senators present concurring,) That the Senate advise and consent to the ratification of the treaty between the United States and the Navajo Indians, concluded at Fort Sumner, New Mexico, on the first day of June, 1868.

Attest:
Geo. C. Gorham
Secretary
By W.J. McDonald
Chief Clerk

Now, therefore, be it known that I, Andrew Johnson, President of the United States of America, do, in pursuance of the advice and consent of the Senate, as expressed in its resolution of the twenty-fifth of July, one thousand eight hundred and sixty-eight, accept, ratify, and confirm the said treaty.

In testimony whereof, I have hereto signed my name, and caused the seal of the United States to be affixed.

Done at the City of Washington. This twelfth day of August, in the year of our Lord one thousand eight hundred and sixty-eight, and of the Independence of the United States of America the ninety-third.

Andrew Johnson
By the President:
W. Hunter
Acting Secretary of State

Leaving Bosque Redondo

On June 18, 1868, my ancestors, the Navajo people, left the Bosque Redondo reservation on their way home to a new Navajo Reservation in their own country. With a column ten miles long that included 7,304 Navajo people, 1500 horses and mules, 2000 sheep, 50 army wagons and four cavalry companies, they walked for six weeks arriving back at their homeland at the end of July. And while it was another long walk, they were happy to be walking after four long years of being imprisoned under miserable conditions.

My great grandparents would have been on the walk and maybe my Grandpa and Grandma. The 1950 census indicates that my Grandpa was 82 and my Grandma was 81 in 1950, but since I do not know their birthdays I don't know if they were born at Bosque Redondo, on the return walk to their own country or shortly after arriving back there. I have a faint memory of Grandma telling me about being born at about the time the tribe had been released from Bosque Redondo, but it is so faint that I'm not even sure if it happened. But it had obviously impacted my Grandma and caused her, because of the way our people had been treated by the white government, to warn us as she told her story, to be wary of trusting white people.

Much of the detail in this chapter comes from the study in preparation for the writing of this book, but the generalities and some of the details I was told by my Grandma, as we sat snug in her hogan, after the sun went down on those cold winter evenings.

The Fort Sumner Historic Site/ Bosque Redondo Memorial now marks the site of this devastating period of Navajo history.

Bosque Redondo Memorial at Fort Sumner, NM.

A message on the wall at Bosque Redondo Memorial reads:

We're still here.
We're surviving.
We didn't get destroyed.
We didn't get erased.
We certainly weren't wiped out.
I think we became stronger

Shonto Begay

During the council proceedings prior to signing the treaty, General Sherman stated that the new reservation contained "about 100 miles square." As of the writing of this book, due primarily to executive actions and acts of Congress, the Navajo reservation contains 27,413 square miles, almost three times the original size.

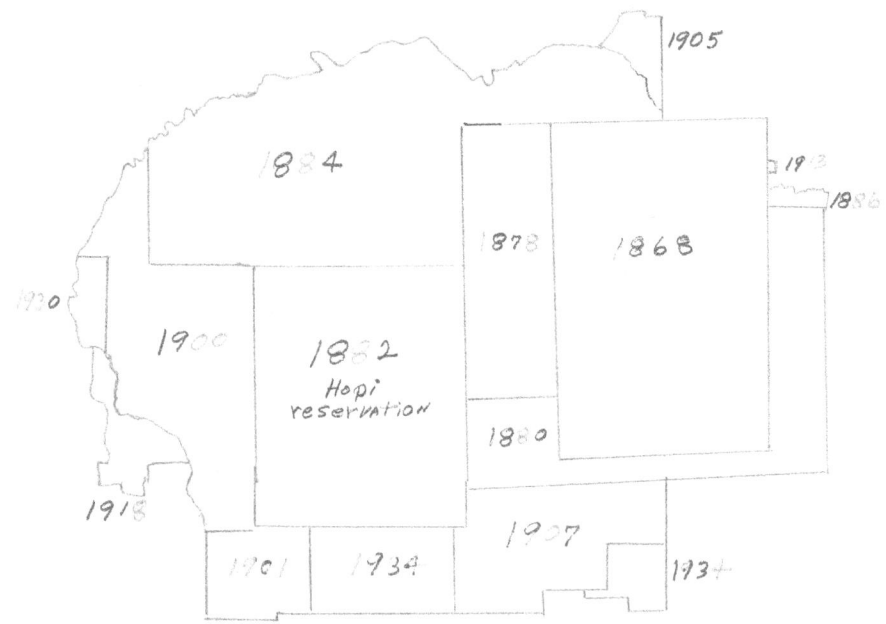

Current Navajo Reservation

CHAPTER 14

Navajo Slavery

Did the enslavement of Navajo women and children really have the impact on Navajo history that we are suggesting it did?

M exico, of which New Mexico and Arizona were a part until the Mexican American War and the Treaty of Guadalupe Hidalgo in 1848, had a checkered history of enslavement of the Indians. In 1493, Pope Alexander VI mandated that the indigenous people were to be converted to Catholicism and that indigenous slavery was prohibited. But there was a catch; if an Indian refused to accept Catholicism, he could be enslaved.

In 1500, Queen Isabella of Spain, who had financed Columbus's voyage to America, ordered that "all the Indians of the Spaniards were to be free from slavery." But when Cortez invaded Mexico, he went back to the loophole put in place by the Pope. In about 1525, the Catholic Church became more involved with an on-again-off-again approach to slavery of the Indians. While the Mexican Constitution enacted in 1824 freed the slaves, it continued in the northern areas that would become part of the United States in 1848. And while not all the Indian slaves were Navajo, it seems a major portion of them were.

It is apparent that Navajo slavery was on the minds of the Chiefs and Headmen who were part of the council held by the Peace Commission with General Sherman and Lt. Colonel Tappan, because that's the only thing they asked of the government other than to be allowed to return to their own country and be allowed to hunt and trade off the reservation. While at first Sherman tried to not deal with that issue adequately, since it was not specifically a part of what they were there to do, he did explain that the country had just fought a civil war over that issue and that slavery had been outlawed. Tappan brought the conversation back to the slavery issue after Sherman switched to talk of the treaty, and tried to get a feel for how big the problem was. That prompted Sherman to explain briefly that slavery was illegal in the United States and there was a legal way to get slaves released.

What he was talking about was the 13th and 14th amendments to the United States Constitution that made slavery illegal in the United States.

Was it correct that over half the Navajo tribe was enslaved at this time? Evidence shows that this estimate was probably close to being correct.

In 1865, hearings on the matter were held at Fort Sumner by a congressional committee dubbed the Doolittle Committee. Several people spoke to the committee, including Juan Baptiste Laney, a Roman Catholic bishop of New Mexico, Arizona and Colorado, who resided there for fourteen years. He said,

> There are a good many Navajo captives among the Mexican families; they make the best of servants. Some families abuse them, while others treat them like their own children. Most of the Mexican families have them; there are more than a thousand of them, perhaps two or three thousand. Part of these captives have been taken in war with the Navajoes (sic) and part have been purchased from the Indians, such as the Utes, who are constantly at war with the Navajoes (sic). These slaves have been bought and sold in this manner for years...

Louis Kennon also gave this sworn testimony:

> Am a resident of New Mexico; have been for twelve years past. I am a native of Georgia; am a physician by pro-

fession. I am tolerably well acquainted with what is called the Navajo country. I think the Navajoes (sic) have been the most abused people on the continent, that in all hostilities the Mexicans have always taken the initiative with but one exception that I know of. When I first came here the Navajoes (sic) were at peace, and had been a long time. … I think the number of Navajo captives held as slaves to be underestimated. I think there are from five to six thousand. I know of no family which can raise one hundred and fifty dollars but what purchases a Navajo slave, and many families own four or five — the trade in them being as regular as the trade in pigs or sheep. Previous to the war their price was from seventy-five to a hundred dollars; but now they are worth about four hundred dollars. But the other day some Mexican Indians from Chihuahua were for sale in Santa Fe. I have been conversant with the institution of slavery in Georgia, but the system is worse here, there being no obligation resting on the owner to care for the slave when he becomes old or worthless.…

It appears that while not dealing seriously with the slavery issue at the time of the treaty negotiations, either Sherman or Tappan must have understood the concerns of the Chiefs and Headmen and taken those concerns back to Congress, because on July 27, 1868, Congress approved the following resolution:

Be it resolved by the Senate and House of Representatives of the United States of America in Congress assembled, That Lieut. Gen. W.T. Sherman be and he is hereby authorized and requested to use the most efficient means his judgment will approve to reclaim from peonage the women and children of the Navajo Indians now held in slavery in the territory adjacent to their homes and the reservation on which the Navajo Indians have been confined."

On September 8, 1868, General Sherman wrote to the commander of the New Mexico district, General Getty, outlining a plan to comply with this resolution. He said, in part,

> By the fourteenth amendment to the constitution of the United States no person can be held as a slave in any part of the United States, but as the language of this resolution is restricted to the 'women and the children' of the Navajo Indians, I infer that the Navajo men restrained of their liberty, either as slaves or as peons, have full protection under a former law, and are construed as perfectly able to take care of themselves without our assistance; but that the women and children so held as slaves, or as peons, need the friendly assistance of the officers of the government.

> In the first place convey to the Navajos themselves the substance of this law, and of our purpose to execute it in the spirit of fairness to them and in justice to the women and children affected. If they as a tribe, or any of them in their private capacities, wish to search for missing women or children, supposed to be held in bondage, you may permit them to make a search and provide for it out of the money held by you on account of the Navajo nation.

> In like manner, if you know or learn of the whereabouts of such women or children, or if any other of your command obtain such knowledge, you or they may act in the manner of guardian to such women or children till they make election to remain where they are or to join their tribe, in which case you may provide for their removal out of the money held by you as described.

> If any woman be married away from her tribe, she should be permitted to have free choice of action. If unmarried and held as a servant, the officer shoud (sic) explain to her, her rights under the law, and leave her free to choose,

satisfying himself that she receives wages and understands her true position.

If children male of (sic) [or] female, under the usual ages of manhood or womanhood, be held as slaves, peons or servants, they should be dealt with according to their age and intelligence. If old enough to form a reasonable judgment of their own interests, they should be allowed to choose their own course; but if too young or too obtuse the officer should himself judge of their true interests. If, on inquiry, their parents can be found, and if they claim the restitution of their children, such restitution must be made without further question.

Whether these orders were actually carried out and how many Navajo slaves were actually returned to the tribe we do not know. I do not remember my grandma, or anyone else for that matter, talking about the Navajo slavery issue. It was not until the research for this book that I became aware of it.

CHAPTER 15

Two Diamonds in the Desert

Hubbell Trading Post

The valley where the Hubbell Trading Post would eventually be located was the home of the band of Navajos led by Chief Ganado Mucho. In about 1874, the federal Indian agent demanded that

Ganado Mucho

Ganado Mucho move his cattle and sheep to a different area. Mucho enlisted the help of War Chief Manuelito, and the two of them rode to Fort Wingate to file a complaint. They decided the best way to do that was to send a petition to the agent's superior, the superintendent for the area, but first they would need to find someone who could write. They found a clerk who would write the petition for them; his name was John Lorenzo Hubbell. From that meeting on, Mucho and Hubbell would become friends.

John Hubbell's mother was of Spanish descent and his father was a Connecticut Yankee. His family, who lived in New Mexico Territory, kept Navajo slaves and often fought against the Navajos (my ancestors) at the time John Hubbell was born. As early as 1851, John Hubbell's father led a posse into Navajo country in search of revenge for livestock that had supposedly been stolen by Navajos. The posse succeeded in destroying the livestock and camp of Chief Manuelito, which was in the valley of Pueblo, Colorado. John Hubbell's uncle had also been

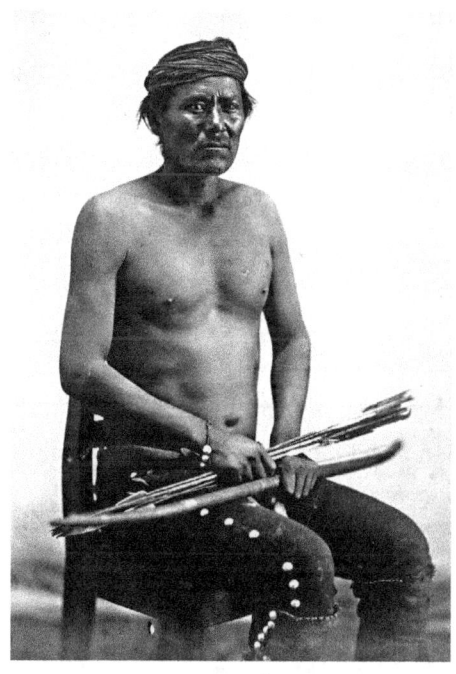

Manuelito

part of Kit Carson's raiders who had fought against the Navajos before the Long Walk.

As a young man, John Hubbell left home and worked as an assistant postmaster in Albuquerque. A year later, this restless young man moved on to Santa Fe and worked as a clerk. By 1870, he was off to the wilds of Utah Territory. Due to having had words with some men in town, he was quickly back on his horse and headed south. The story is told of how he was followed by seven men, whom he outsmarted. He ended up killing all seven, but was wounded in the process. He made his way to the Grand Canyon, and as the story goes, was nursed back to health by Paiute Indians.

Five years later, he rode into Fort Defiance and was hired as a clerk to inventory the Navajo annuity goods provided by the 1868 Treaty. Within a short time, he moved on to Fort Wingate. It was here that he assisted Ganado Mucho and Manuelito with their petition and where the unlikely friendship between John Hubbell and Ganado Mucho began.

In 1878, John Lorenzo Hubbell established the Hubbell Trading Post on the Navajo reservation by purchasing an existing trading post from his competitor, William Leonard. (My ancestors were among those Navajo people. They had come to their newly established reservation just a few years earlier from their confinement at Bosque Redondo reservation.)

Being an entrepreneur, Hubbell saw an opportunity. This would be his second trading post, his first one being near Ganado Lake, which he was forced to close because a man suspected of being a witch was killed in the doorway of his trading post and thereafter no Navajo would enter because the building was cursed. He established his home on this newly purchased land and he would live there for about 50 years.

Hubbell Trading Post

Hubbell encouraged my ancestors to make silver jewelry, Navajo rugs and baskets to exchange for money and groceries at his trading post. As a matter of fact, he paid them with tin coins that could only be spent at his trading post. He supported those who were supplying this merchandise, especially the artwork that he sold to tourists. A settlement soon grew up around the trading post.

Soon he was trading in wool, sheep, corn and pinion nuts in addition to the Indian's artwork, and the trading post became the center of community activities. My ancestors would gather at the trading post to tell stories, discuss the issues of the day, gamble, and participate in the "chicken pull" games sponsored by Hubbell. The "chicken pull" was kind of a cross between a rodeo game and a polo match, but in those days, they used a live chicken. Winners got prizes.

A good example of the happenings at the Hubbell Trading Post occurred the night after the white doctor, Dr. Clarence Salsbury, operated on a young Navajo girl's broken leg only to have a blood clot take her life during surgery. The girl's parents and others gathered at the trading post to talk about revenge. Dr. Salsbury's life was in danger until a Navajo medicine man intervened in defense of the white doctor. (Dr. Salsbury was primarily responsible for development of the Presbyterian mission in Ganado and the hospital that became Sage Memorial Hospital.) On that particular night, the medicine man probably saved his life. The Indians didn't forget this death though, and the number of patients he was asked to treat suffered for months.

John Hubbell spoke three languages, English, Navajo and Spanish, which made him able to communicate effectively with most people in the area. He changed his first name from John to Juan or Don, depending on who he was talking with. His business flourished and allowed him to expand his empire to a variety of different businesses. He also provided jobs for many of the Navajo people.

John Lorenzo Hubbell

He became popular enough to enter Arizona Territory politics. He was, at one time or another, on the Board of Jail Commissioners, the Sheriff, and later in the Arizona Territorial Legislature. There were also times when he was hated, especially during the range wars between the Texas cattlemen and the New Mexican and Navajo sheepherders.

John Hubbell was a man on the go. Since his wife did not live at the trading post, he was free to travel for business or womanizing. His trading post was a stopping off point for many prominent people, including every United States president from Cleveland to Harding.

It was Hubbell that convinced the people of the area around his trading post to name the town Ganado in honor of his Navajo friend, Ganado Mucho. The story is that Hubbell's Trading Post was the post office for the community, and the address was Pueblo Colorado, Arizona Territory. That confused the postal delivery and much mail was mis-delivered to the town of Pueblo in the state of Colorado. The problem was solved by renaming the town, Ganado.

Sometimes with the luxuries that we all enjoy today, it is hard to imagine what life was like in the "Wild West." I am quoting from Jim Kristofic's excellent and well researched book, *Medicine Women,* as evidence that what I mentioned earlier in this chapter is most likely true:

> While working to guide the new Sage Memorial Hospital to its finish that spring, Salsbury made regular visits across the wash to treat Hubbell. The man once taken as a dead ringer for a robust Teddy Roosevelt was now more than seventy years old. His white hair and mustache had thinned to wisps, and he squinted through thick wire-rimmed glasses. Hands that had once gripped leather reins during the chicken-pulls and long rides between trading posts were now dark with liver spots and clutched weakly at the blanket that wrapped over his legs. He didn't use his legs often anymore. He mostly moved around the yard of the trading post by wheelchair now.
>
> One cold November morning, as Salsbury touched his stethoscope to the pale flesh of the old man's chest, and Hubbell leaned toward Salsbury and whispered, "Doctor Tso, do you believe in the Bible where it says that they that live by the sword shall die by the sword?"
>
> "Why, Don Lorenzo?" Salsbury asked.

Then the old man pulled up his shirt and showed Salsbury something he would always remember. A pale scar running along the left flank of his abdomen looked like he had been gored by a bull horn or a bowie knife. Hubbell spoke in whispers of his travels into Utah. He talked about the ambush and gunfight with seven men, his swim on the Colorado River, and his rescue by a band of Paiute Indians.

In 1930, John Lorenzo Hubbell died at age 77 and was buried at Hubbell Hill, close to the trading post. His wife and his good friend Manyhorses, son of Ganado Mucho, are buried next to him. He created an empire during his life, that included a dozen or more trading posts. After John Hubbell's death, his children commissioned stone mason Emillo Limas to build a stone hogan as a memorial to their father and his hospitality. It memorializes the fact that John Hubbell would welcome people from all walks of life to his trading post and his home.

Left, Hubbell Hill, gravesite of John Lorenzo Hubbell, his wife and Manyhorses, son of Ganado Mucho.

Right, Memorial hogan with gravesite in the distance to the right of hogan.

With John Lorenzo Hubbell gone, his son, Roman, and his wife, Dorothy, took over operation of the trading posts for the next twenty or so years. Time eventually took its toll and Roman suffered a stroke that confined him to a wheelchair. By 1957, the Hubbell Trading post was put up for sale — all of the other businesses had been sold or closed. (There may have been a bankruptcy somewhere in the process.) While some prospective buyers wanted to liquidate the antiques and artifacts at the trading post, Dorothy wanted the trading post to remain intact.

National Historic Site Established

When the idea of turning the property into a National Historic Site surfaced, Ted Danson's father, Ned Danson, took the lead. He soon solicited the help of Senators Barry Goldwater and Carl Hayden, as well as Congressman Stewart Udall. Both Udall and Hayden had met the elderly John Lorenzo, and Barry Goldwater had played with Hubbell's children in 1916 when he was a child.

On May 7, 1959, Senator Haydon introduced legislation in the Senate that would purchase the site for $300,000 and Congressman Udall did likewise in the house. Senate bill S.1871 passed in the senate, but the house bill was defeated because the $300,000 purchase price was thought to be excessive. Five years later, new legislation was introduced that would preserve the site, and have it operating as a live trading post complete with a genuine Indian trader. The measure passed and President Lyndon Johnson signed it on August 28, 1965.

The purchase was finalized in 1967, with the Southwest Parks and Monuments Association, a non-profit organization, chosen to operate the trading post. The Southwest Parks and Monuments Association had been organized to help the National Park Service with educational, scientific, historical and interpretive activities. So, that same year the National Park Service took over the operation of the Hubbell Trading Post and it was designated a National Historic Site.

Hubbell Trading Post, National Historic Site.

The first trader hired to run the historic post was Bill Young. He ran the post until he retired in 1978. Al Grieve then ran it until 1981, when Billy Malone was asked to apply for the job.

A bit about Billy Malone

Billy Malone was born in 1939 in Gallup, New Mexico. When his parents divorced, he moved with his family to Colorado and in 1958 he joined the army. By the time he was discharged, his mother had married Hugh Lee, an old-time trader from Ganado and this is how Billy got to the Ganado area.

Al Frick gave him a job working at the Lupton Trading Post and before long, Minnie Goodluck, a beautiful Navajo girl, came into his life. They were married in 1962. By this time, Billy's stepfather was working for Cliff McGee at Keams Canyon, so Billy and Minnie moved to Keams Canyon.

Before long, McGee offered Billy a job working at the Pinon Trading Post, which was also owned by the McGee family. Billy worked there for 18 years. During this time, he and Minnie had five children — four girls and one boy. He eventually became the head Indian trader there.

Pinon, located about 50 miles west of Chinle, was pretty remote and primitive. Travel was mostly by horses and wagon on a dirt road, which was the only access to Keams Canyon. During the time Billy worked for the McGee family, Minnie had become a successful silversmith and weaver, in addition to being the local postmaster. The Malone family had a good, comfortable life, so it was not an easy decision for Billy to apply for the Hubbell job. He and Minnie talked it over and decided that he should apply.

Some eight or ten applicants had already applied for the position, but about 15 minutes after Billy Malone's interview was done, he was offered the job. He was one of the most experienced, respected and trusted Indian traders on the Navajo Reservation and the National Park Service and the Southwest Parks and Monuments Association were very pleased with their choice.

My Hubbell Trading Post Job

When I walked into the Hubbell Trading Post and asked for a job, Bill Malone was the one who interviewed me and he hired me on the spot. I had been doing some silver-smithing and I knew about Navajo rugs from my family, so I could talk confidently to prospective customers. Apparently, that was enough qualification for Bill, and I spent the rest of that same day working at the Post.

I worked there for five or six years, primarily selling Navajo rugs and silver jewelry to the customers who visited the Post. Every day brought people who were enamored by what I had to show them: beautiful Ganado Red rugs; amazing turquoise jewelry—much of it pawn. I also told them the stories of how they had been painstakingly made.

During my time at Hubbell's, I showed many beautiful rugs to customers. When they decided they wanted to purchase a particular rug, Bill would step in and finalize the deal.

Jewelry and rugs were my specialty. I was already managing the Exxon gas station and small store in Ganado. This was a station in the old style, with an attendant who pumped the gas, checked the oil and washed the windows for each customer. That attendant was sometimes me! (During the time when I was manager of the station, I hired a young man named Manley, who would eventually become my common law husband.)

I loved working at the Hubbell Trading Post and I loved managing the Exxon station. I was a busy lady with two jobs and a growing family to take care of. Working for Billy Malone was an awesome experience. He would go out of his way to help his customers, and he would help anybody that needed it — often extending them credit until their rug or jewelry was completed. He also sometimes reached into his own pocket to help out a Navajo who needed a few dollars.

He was kind of a father figure to many of his customers — maybe to me as well, for obvious reasons. His customer base continued to grow because people knew they could expect a fair deal. Working at Hubbell I loved hearing the stories about John Hubbell and they gave me great guidance in the ways of business. They also planted the seed of desire to start something of my own.

John Hubbell had once said, "I know a lot of people have the idea that an Indian trader is a first-class scoundrel — a man who attains financial prosperity by fleecing the Indians. There may have been some that have, but they didn't last long. I've been an Indian trader for fifty years, but I've dealt honestly with them. I've never taken a dollar from an Indian without giving the Indian value received, and I've often given the Indians what should have been my own legitimate margin of business profit just to help them when they need it."

During a 1998 interview and as the manager of the Hubbell Trading Post, Billy Malone was asked what the attributes of a good Indian trader are. Very much in the spirit of John Lorenzo Hubbell he answered that the three attributes of a good Indian trader are most importantly honesty, followed by benevolence and being of good-natured disposition. That was the Billy Malone (we called him Bill at work) that I knew.

Ganado Mission

Those in charge of Presbyterian church missions had decided to establish a Presbyterian mission on the Navajo Reservation and like most others who visited the area, their first stop was at the Hubbell Trading Post. John Hubbell greeted them warmly, as he did most visitors, and that welcome plus the availability of water, land capable of growing crops and the availability of building materials sealed the deal. And so, in 1901 the Ganado Mission was founded.

Under the leadership of Rev Charles Bierkemper, the first building was erected, *Old Manse*, in 1903 which served as living quarters for the Bierkemper family as well as a meeting hall and a classroom for the new day school. Next a school building and dormitories were built and soon after, in 1906, the Ganado Mission Church.

With the arrival of Dr James Kennedy, the first hospital was established in 1911, and with the arrival of Rev. Fred Mitchell in 1920, the mission had its first superintendent.

Mission Presbyterian Church ruins.

The mission already had a good start when Dr. Clarence Salsbury arrived in 1927. Dr. Salsbury, just like Dr. Kennedy before him, saw many of his patients at their scattered hogans, and if he felt the patient needed to be hospitalized, he would have to convince the parents, and often the medicine man, to allow him to treat the patient at the hospital. That was the case when he convinced the parents of a young girl that her seriously fractured leg needed surgical correction in order to heal properly. The parents reluctantly agreed. As surgery proceeded a blood clot suddenly ended the young girl's life, and what ensued not only almost ended Dr. Salsbury's career as a doctor but perhaps his life. That evening many Navajos gathered at the Hubbell Trading Post as they often did, and along with the deceased girl's parents, the conversation quickly went to what revenge was appropriate for Dr Salsbury's terrible act. As the conversation grew heated, a respected Navajo medicine man stood to say that he too had been in situations where even with his best intentions, the patient died. Go home, he said. They did and Dr Salsbury was spared.

Despite the rough start the people of the area slowly gained confidence in Dr Salsbury and the mission hospital. By 1930 Dr Salisbury's dream of a nursing school for Indian girls and other minorities became a reality. Dr Salsbury wrote in his memoirs, "lots of people said that girls with red skins would never be able to handle the academic subjects, could not master the surgical techniques and most emphatically would never touch a dead body. I was told a thousand times that Indians were just not temperamentally suited to be nurses." Dr Salsbury ignored their warning and by 1945 when the graduating class from the Ganado Nursing School took the board examination for licensing, they got the best scores of any nursing school and one girl, who happened to be one of the Japanese interned during WWII, got a perfect score.

But from that point on the nursing education at Ganado School of Nursing rapidly declined to the point where only a few of the graduates in 1947 were able to pass the examining board test. As time went on it had become harder and harder to find qualified nursing teachers who were willing to endure the low wages and hardships of working at the Ganado School of Nursing and due to changing attitudes within the Presbyterian

Church it became difficult to convince them of the need for more money. Consequently, the nursing students were being short changed.

Sort of like John Hubbell, Dr Salsbury was a showman and a promoter and had a way of convincing people that his mission at Ganado was worth entrusting their dollars to. For several years he organized what he called a Chautauqua, which he described as "part revival meeting, part medical clinic, part county fair, and part adult education course." He was in a way competing with the sings of the medicine men but he got away with it by involving the Navajo people in his Chautauqua. In addition to seminars where visiting doctors from across the region would read their papers, there were talks by Navajo attendees like former tribal council chairman Chee Dodge as well as baseball games and foot races and lots of food. These events would last for 2 or 3 days and drew crowds from across the area and departing doctors would often leave sizable donations as they left in support the mission.

When John Collier and the Bureau of Indian Affairs under President Franklin Roosevelt took office, they were instrumental in starting what was named the Navajo Nation Fair, which they scheduled to immediately follow Dr Salsbury's Chautauqua. The fair became very popular and so partly because of the competition for attendees but partly in an effort to save money, the Chautauqua ended.

By 1950 Dr Clarence Salsbury was ready to turn the reins of the Ganado Mission over to someone else, partly because of the allergies he had developed to the trees he had overseen the planting of at the mission. And so, on May 25, 1950 he said goodbye to the dream he'd had and the mission he had created since 1927, and turned the mission over to Dr Joseph Poncel. For 23 years he had attended to even the tiniest detail of the functioning of the mission and through his network of donors had caused it to become the largest Indian mission in United States history.

But the School of Nursing that a few years earlier had been at the very top, was in trouble, and it was eventually closed on May 5, 1951, primarily because of lack of funding caused at least partially by the federal government's program of government run Indian hospitals, which it was difficult for a private hospital to compete against, but also because of the changing attitudes of the Presbyterian church toward funding missions.

So, by the time I was ready to enter the medical field, the school of nursing was long gone. As the Ganado public school grew, the government school was closed, and as the mission school enrollment declined, it was replaced with the College of Ganado. By 1969, Project H.O.P.E., an international health care organization founded in the United States in 1958, was working with Navajo leaders and would eventually help establish the first native American operated health care system in the United States. I enrolled in the nurse's aide training program at College of Ganado and graduated from that course of study. Whether Project H.O.P.E. was involved with my studies I do not know.

Jim Kristofic in his book *Medicine Women* writes, "The mission, which had become the largest Indian mission in United States history ... outgrew the Church's ability to pay for it. The Board of National Missions chaotically heaved the campus and the hospital over to Project H.O.P.E."

On August 5, 2009, Ray Kersting wrote "Ganado Presbyterian Mission's Sage Memorial Hospital School of Nursing has been named a National Historic Landmark by the National Park Service. A special recognition ceremony will be held by Grand Canyon Presbytery ... on the afternoon of Sept. 19 to recognize the honor and to dedicate a Landmark Garden. Three monuments are planned for the garden along with four mahogany granite benches. The site will provide a tranquil place for visitors to sit among flora found in the early Mission garden. Donations are being accepted by the Presbytery to cover the cost."

I faintly remember the benches from my time at College of Ganado but had no idea of its significance.

***

On one side of the wash, was the diamond created by John Lorenzo Hubbell, where he established a business to act as a market for my ancestor's goods and a store where they could buy the provisions they needed. But it was more than that. It was a gathering place for the community as well as a destination for travelers. Hubbell had built four Hogan's outside his trading post to be used by weary travelers and he provided entertainment for the locals gathered after the workday was completed, Life was not easy in Arizona territory, and later the State of Arizona, in those days, but Hubbell found a way to cope and to survive and a way to gain an appreciation for the Navajo way of life to which they reciprocated. And it was successful enough that he created an empire, an empire that would disappear with the second generation except for the Trading Post which would eventually be recognized as significant enough to be designated a National Historic Site. Truly a Ganado diamond in the desert.

On the other side of the wash, a diamond created a little later, primarily by Dr Clarence Salsbury, was the Ganado Mission, a mission dedicated to health, education and Christianity. In a lot of ways, like John Hubbell, he was an organizer and a showman. Salsbury convinced donors to fund what he would develop into the largest Indian mission in United States history. His mission for a few years was the center of modern medicine in the area, and he proved the naysayers wrong when his nursing school graduates scored the highest on board exams of any nursing school in Arizona. He too built a hogan outside the hospital for the use of relatives of patients. Salsbury too created an empire, an empire confined to the 160 acres that the Presbyterian mission owned, but none the less a magnificent empire in the desert, an oasis of sorts. Jim Kristofic in his book *Medicine Women*, describes it this way, "Here it was in Ganado mission: living proof that a Christian way of life could bring forth the blossoms of modern medicine, education, and religion to a group of people who—two generations prior—had been at war with the United States." And while John Hubbell's heirs eventually sold or closed the properties John Hubbell had amassed, the Presbyterian church essentially just walked away from the mission. In 2009 Sage Memorial Hospital and the School of Nursing was made a National Historic Landmark. Truly a Ganado diamond in the desert.

Monument on the former Ganada Mission grounds, left.

Monument message, below.

DEDICATED TO THE MEMORY OF THOSE WHO MADE THE SUPREME SACRIFICE AND IN HONOR OF THOSE WHO SERVED IN THE ARMED FORCES OF OUR COUNTRY WORLD WAR II

REPRESENTING

GANADO MISSION'S STAFF HIGH SCHOOL AND SCHOOL OF NURSING

CHAPTER 16

The Diamonds Lose Their Luster

Hubbell Trading Post

My (Verna's) visit with Billy Malone and his canine friend.

It had been many years since I had worked for Billy Malone at the Hubbell Trading Post; many years since my career path had taken me away from selling jewelry and Navajo rugs to my chosen career in health care. Then a few months ago while visiting with my brother Lynn and my Uncle Joe in Gallup, New Mexico, they took me to Billy Malones store in Gallup. While it took a few minutes for memories to resurface, we had a cordial and fun time reminiscing in between customers.

Before I left, Bill Malone we always called him at work, gave me a copy of the book, *The Case of the Indian Trader* which is the story of what the federal government bureaucracy did to him. On the way home I thought to myself, I wish I had known. At the very least I could have offered a word of support, because I knew the Billy Malone they were describing was not the Billy Malone that I knew.

The sun had not yet started to peek over the horizon when a loud pounding on the front door of his house aroused Billy Malone from a deep sleep. He hurriedly pulled on a pair of pants and unlocked the front door only to be greeted by federal agents. Being still not completely awake he was shown a warrant that authorized the agents to close the trading post down for three days and seize the financial records as evidence that Malone had been forging documents and was embezzling funds from the trading post.

Billy, his wife Minnie and his mother-in-law, who was staying with them temporarily while she recovered from a heart attack, were ordered not to leave the house. The National Park Service and the Western

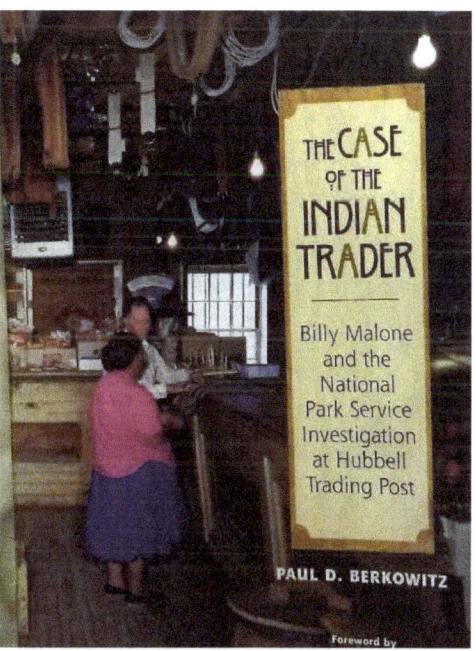

Book by Paul D. Berkowitz.

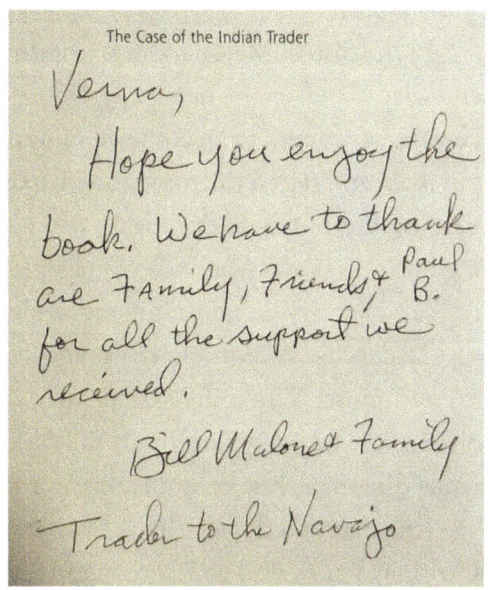

The message Bill Malone wrote in the copy of the book he gave me.

National Parks Association apparently thought Malone was cheating them out of funds that were rightfully theirs.

Billy Malone was a traditional Indian trader, the very thing that had caused the board of directors to so hurriedly hire him ahead of other applicants who had applied first. In order to understand this fiasco, one has to understand what a traditional Indian trader is, or was. Most traditional trading posts were in remote areas of the reservation that didn't have the availability of a bank and a grocery store and a hardware store or a community center or a place to market their livestock or crops or other things they had to sell. So, the trader acted as their bank and they could get a loan by pawning the turquoise bracelet on their wrist without the many pages of paperwork and the delay in approval that they would encounter if they were to make the effort to go off the reservation to a bank.

They probably knew that Malone seldom sold their pawned items when they became dead pawns, so they might still be reclaimed months or years later. The trading post was also the place where they could often get an advance on the rug they were weaving that wouldn't be finished for a few months.

In the case of Malone, it was not unusual for him to reach in his pocket and give a person in need a few dollars.. A good trader encouraged his Navajo customers to make jewelry and weave rugs which he would then purchase and sell to the tourists who would frequent the trading post. Also, because the Hubbell Trading Post was a tourist destination with a thriving business under Malone's management, many other traders would place rugs and jewelry on consignment at Hubbell as well.

Traders like Malone acted as businessmen, educators, counselors, bankers and more. While the system may have seemed chaotic to the outside observer, it was very orderly in Billy Malone's head. He may not have had fancy diplomas, but he was brilliant at this.

Isn't that exactly what Ned Danson and Senators Barry Goldwater and Carl Hayden as well as Representative Stewart Udall had promoted when they lobbied for preserving the Hubbell Trading Post as a National Historic Site? Didn't the bill that Congress passed and President Lyndon Johnson signed in 1965 authorize not only the preservation of the trading post but that it would be operated as a "living" trading post with a "genuine Indian trader?"

The Southwestern Parks and Monuments Association was chosen to take over operation of the trading post. Jim Babbitt, brother of Bruce Babbitt, was chairman of the executive committee and LeeAnn Simpson was the executive director. As time went on, they both departed from the language of the bill congress had passed and started finding fault with the way trader Malone was operating the post.

Babbitt wanted to dictate who Malone did business with and Simpson wanted the operation to fit into the government balance sheets. At times, it seemed that Simpson was just plain vindictive and out to "get" Billy Malone. Plus, Babbitt was upset that Malone wouldn't abandon his long-term source for Pendleton blankets in favor of one in which Babbitt had a financial interest. The federal government bureaucracy was once again at odds with the intent of Congress.

As the federal agents searched Malone's house for the financial records they sought, it was impossible not to notice the stacks of Navajo rugs and the boxes of baskets and silver jewelry that he had stored there. While their search warrant was only for financial records,, they made the erroneous, illegal and foolish decision to confiscate all of these rugs, jewelry and baskets. In their mind it must have seemed obvious that all of this stuff was stolen property and must rightfully belong to the association they served.

Within a week Billy Malone was fired from his job as trader and ordered to vacate his government-provided house. Not really knowing what was happening, he swallowed his pride and moved in with his daughter and her family in Gallup, New Mexico. The trading post was shut down and the employees were sent home with little or no explanation. Within a few days Billy and Minnie Malone's life savings, along with their residence and Billy's job, were taken away from them. The stress of this almost killed Billy.

Almost two years passed and Malone had still not been charged with anything. By a stroke of luck for Billy Malone, the investigation was turned over to a thorough, honest and by-the-book investigator who was almost retirement age. Paul D. Berkowitz was told that too much money and time had already been spent on the case and they didn't care what the charges were, they just wanted Malone arrested. Berkowitz started his investigation with the belief that Malone was guilty, but after viewing the sloppiness of the previous investigators, the number of important investigations and interviews that had not been done and the doubtful legality of some of their actions, he was beginning to have doubts.

Some of the people the previous investigators had attempted to interview refused to talk to them simply because of the unfriendly way they were asked, and others refused because they knew how honest a man Malone was. This all changed with Berkowitz.

It was most likely the multiple interviews with Billy Malone that made Berkowitz truly doubt that this man had committed the crimes he was accused of committing. But Berkowitz, unlike his predecessors on the case, still conducted a methodical and thorough investigation What he witnessed was Malone, without hesitation, answering each of his questions, as well as readily agreeing to a polygraph test.

Berkowitz also saw that the seizure of Malone's property, instead of just the financial records, had clearly been done without a valid search warrant. With the evidence he gathered, Berkowitz made the only decision he could legally make—Malone's property, which had been stored in a government vault in Tucson where it had been placed after it had all been frozen to kill any possible insect infestation, must be returned to him.

If Berkowitz had any further doubts, they evaporated as he watched Malone spend hours identifying each rug, basket and piece of jewelry and give an explanation of which were a part of his personal collection, which were pieces his wife Minnie had made and which pieces were being held on consignment for some other trader.

When he was finished, Malone made it known that there were a few pieces missing. The most notable was an important basket and a box that contained cash and checks. Eventually, the pressure got too great and the missing items were found and returned to Malone.

LeAnn Simpson was angry at how things were going, and Berkowitz was accused of switching teams. Apparently, a deal had been made between Simpson's Western National Parks Association and the National Park Service, that in a nutshell said, the Western National Parks Association would provide funding for the investigation of Malone in return for a promise that they would get all of Malone's seized property.

Berkowitz's investigation continued, with each facet ending with a finding of no chargeable crime. The only possible crime was the accusation of endorsing checks made out to someone else, which he freely admitted to. Most of those checks were made out to his daughter or son-in-law, who both had given him money to invest in rugs for them with the instructions that he should cash the checks and reinvest the money by buying more rugs. Even with that admission, the handwriting experts could not confirm that the endorsements were actually in Malone's handwriting.

I feel obligated to quote from *The Case of the Indian Trader* by federal investigator turned author Paul D. Berkowitz because it is so poignant and reveals the honest and gentle man that Malone was and is.

"I pulled Malone aside, handed him the letter, and told him, 'It's over.' The NPS [National Park Service] investigation and the government's case against you is closed.

"Malone's eyes welled up as he read the letter. He reached out to shake my hand, quietly saying, 'thank you,' and then gave me a hug. It was one of the most remarkable and gratifying moments I had experienced in my entire thirty-three-year career."

This case turned Berkowitz into a whistle-blower. His report to the Office of Inspector General at the Department of the Interior resulted in the people who had botched the Hubbell investigation in the first place being charged with the same crime they had accused Billy Malone of, 18 USC 1001 (false statements), a federal crime.

Unfortunately the federal bureaucracy has not changed as a result of this revelation. It is still burdened with corruption, fraud and incestuous appointments.

What this case did accomplish, probably not intentionally because I don't think they knew what a real Indian trading post was, is to destroy the intent of Congress when it passed the law saying that the Hubbell Trading Post would be operated as a "living" trading post with a "genuine Indian trader." Billy Malone was the last of the genuine Indian traders at Hubbell Trading Post. It's now just another tourist souvenir shop at an historic site. The luster was gone from this diamond in the desert.

Ganado Mission

The Ganado Mission truly was a jewel—a diamond in the desert. It was a mission project started by the Presbyterian Church in 1901, and by 1906, the Ganado Presbyterian Church had been established. The 160-acre mission grounds slowly developed in the beginning. They needed to find water and they needed to build buildings, first under the leadership of Rev. Charles Bierkemper.

The first hospital was built in 1911 when Dr James Kennedy arrived at the mission. The glory days of the mission started with the arrival of Dr. Clarence Salsbury, a charismatic promoter with a bit of a showman's flair. He could convince people to part with their money, both Presbyterian church members and others.

He also proved that those who said Indian women could never accomplish nursing skills were wrong, and he rubbed dirt in their faces by graduating a class of nurses in 1945 that scored the highest on the licensing examination of any nursing school taking the test.

Each year Dr Salsbury held what he called a Chautauqua at the mission, where doctors from around the area would present their papers combined with the involvement of the Navajo people and lots of food and games. Navajo people from across the area showed up for the festivities.

But it was getting harder and harder to get good teachers for the nursing school—teachers who were willing to sacrifice the larger salaries they could get elsewhere and teach in the remoteness of the desert. Because of this, test scores started to decline to the point where most nursing graduates from the mission nursing school could not pass the license exams.

Then with the appointment of John Collier as the Commissioner of the Bureau of Indian Affairs and with President Roosevelt's New Deal, the Navajo Nation Fair was started. It met immediately following Salsbury's Chautauqua, and that took away many of the participants. Also, under John Collier, the Indian Health Service started taking patients away from the private Ganado Mission hospital.

After 23 years, during which Ganado Mission reached its pinnacle, Dr. Salsbury turned the leadership over to Dr. Poncel in 1950. But the handwriting was already on the wall and the School of Nursing was closed in either 1951 or 1953. With Dr Salsbury's departure, some of the funds that he had kept coming in through his charisma, dried up.

Perhaps the most important reason the mission was in trouble was because of changes in the attitudes of the Presbyterian Church. The church was being fragmented by differing views on the war in Vietnam, the civil rights movement in the South, the ordination of women and the American Indian Movement. With all of that, the church mission, which had created the largest mission in United States history at Ganado, had outgrown the church's ability to pay for it.

Probably because of all of the afore mentioned reasons, the Presbyterian Church Mission Board abandoned the Ganado Mission and turned it over to Project H.O.P.E., which according to Dr Salsbury who was now the director of the Arizona Department of Health, was a stupid idea. He was probably right.

The Presbyterian church still owns the 160-acre property which it leases to the Navajo Health Service. Sadly, the Presbyterian Ganado Mission, in all its glory, no longer exists. This diamond in the desert has lost its luster and no longer shines.

My coauthor, Clare Fitz, thought a picture of the Landmark Garden described in Chapter 15 would be a fitting conclusion to this chapter. This is his account of what he found when he went in search of that Garden.

> Somewhere in my research I had read that a stone bench area had been built on the mission grounds where one could relax and reflect on the days of the mission.

Something told me that it was close to the Presbyterian church. Since I was planning to search for it, my coauthor, Verna, told me that you had to enter a gate to get onto the mission grounds, but that they would let me in.

So, I was not surprised to find a guard shack at the entrance and to have a guard come out to allow me in. The guard seemed to have no knowledge of the aforementioned benches but allowed me to proceed.

As I came to a dead end and started to turn right, a security guard quite a ways down the street motioned me to do something, which I took to mean that I couldn't come that way. I knew they were building a new Sage Memorial Hospital there, so I assumed he was motioning me away from the construction zone

So, I turned left instead. That took me to a church. I parked and made my way down the sidewalk to the rear of the church, and sure enough, there were the stone benches I had come to find. After I had taken some pictures and was walking around to the front of the church, I was met by the security guard.

I told him that I had come in search of the stone bench memorial, and he responded by telling me that the pastor might know what I was looking for and his car was in the lot, so he must be in the church. He pounded on the door of the sanctuary but got no response. So, he went to a side entrance door and knocked. This time, the pastor answered the door.

The security guard brought the pastor over to where I was standing and then went back to his car where he stood and watched us. The pastor was full of knowledge about the days when the mission functioned. Each time I mentioned some happening I had read about, he would show me where it took place, each time with in-depth knowledge.

He also led me back to the stone benches I had come to find. He explained that originally there had been a fountain in the center and four stone benches surrounding it. However, the whole setting had fallen into disrepair and the fountain was no longer functional and in a state of disintegration. Two of the benches no longer had a stone across the top to sit on.

When I mentioned reading about the young men cutting the stone from a local quarry to build the church that we stood beside, he corrected me and took me to the site of the original church which is located behind the current church and is now in a state of ruin.

It was probably the picture I took of the original church the security guard saw and as we walked back to the front of the church, he motioned for the pastor to come and talk to him. The pastor was told that he shouldn't let me take pictures there. I easily solved this by only taking pictures when I was out of the security guard's view.

We talked for fifteen or twenty minutes as the pastor pointed out the original well that had made the lush mission possible and the two canals that were now pretty much filled in from Ganado Lake. Ganado Lake is only about fifty feet higher in elevation than the Ganado Mission and the Hubbell Trading Post, but that was enough to allow water to flow two miles from the lake to the trading post and mission.

As we walked, he pointed out each building that was a part of the original mission. He pointed to the building that housed the boiler that generated the steam which was pumped through underground pipes to each of the buildings. He also told me how a pipe that ran under the new church had at one point burst, releasing steam into the building and essentially destroying the sanctuary.

After a thoroughly enjoyable hour, I bid the pastor a warm farewell and left the mission grounds. The guards could now relax and the pastor and his wife could continue preparing for the church services the next morning. As I waved to the security guard and exited the mission grounds, I thought to myself, *So much for "a tranquil place for visitors to sit among flora found in the early Mission garden."*

This diamond in the desert has truly lost its luster.

The Landmark Garden in ruin.

Salsbury Hall

Ganado Lake

CHAPTER 17

John Collier, the Goat Hater

John Collier, Commissioner of Indian Affairs.

When the 1868 treaty was signed that returned my ancestors from Bosque Redondo to their homelands and the Navajo Reservation was established, they were provided, assuming that the treaty was complied with, fifteen thousand sheep and goats and five hundred beef cattle. By the early 1930's those 15,000 sheep and goats had multiplied to about 2 million.

William Zeh who was a forester for the Navajo Reservation stated in a report in 1930 that the grazing lands were being over grazed and this was causing erosion that threatened to destroy them. He reportedly suggested a minor reduction in the size of the flocks, especially the goats who would eat the entire plant, roots and all.

What alternative did the Navajo have? They were at the mercy of the Federal Government in regard to the size of their reservation and each family only had the 160 acres they had been allocated by the treaty. Yet their flocks of sheep were not only their wealth but their existence as food, wool for clothing and rugs, sinew for thread and for sale in order to purchase other needed goods, even an integral part of their ceremonies so much a part of their religion; essentially the basis of their existence.

But in an article entitled *Indians at Work* written by Commissioner of Indian Affairs John Collier, he wrote,

> The crisis consists in the fact that the soil of the Navajo Reservation is hurriedly being washed away into the Colorado River.
>
> Soil erosion ... due to extreme overgrazing had totally destroyed several thousand acres of the Navajo range. It had seriously damaged millions of acres more.

The Navajo Reservation was being washed into the Boulder Dam (Hoover Dam) reservoir. Actually, the government thought two thirds of the silt being fed to this dam was being washed from the Navajo lands.

In July of 1933 a meeting was held with the Navajo Council at Fort Wingate, and some 2000 Navajos showed up. The solution reached at this meeting was that hundreds of thousands of sheep and goats must disappear. The federal government would not pay for this, so the Navajo had to pay with labor and money.

John Collier's comments regarding this matter,

> Mandatory sheep and goat reduction, mandatory range control, federal dominance over the Navajos present and future program, are already, possible in law and might be justified from the standpoint of national necessity.
>
> But the Navajos were expressly and formally told that compulsion would not be used. This problem was their own and they, not the government, must do the things necessary to its solution.

That was a mixed message, but what they were really saying is that we, the federal government, will not force you to do it as long as you do what we want you to do.

The federal government used the tribal council and the chapter houses as front men as they tried to get approval from the people. There was obviously opposition. It is not exactly clear what went on, but by some method sheep, goat, cattle and horse populations were being drastically reduced.

What Happened as a Result of this Mandatory Reduction

Chester Nez, one of the original code talkers, remembers what happened to his grandma's sheep and goats when he was a young boy of thirteen or fourteen.

It was late summer and he would soon be going off to boarding school at Fort Defiance when he heard a rumble coming down the road, and in anticipation watched as a flatbed truck hauling a large bulldozer stopped at his grandma's place. As they unloaded the bulldozer, these two Navajo men told us that they worked for the Bureau of Indian Affairs, government workers.

The large machine lumbered across his grandma's land to a location in front of his grandma's hogan where they started digging a long trench about 150 feet long and 4 or 5 feet deep.

They then moved on to our neighbor's property and did the same thing there until there were three or four trenches besides the one at our place. Chester wrote that he wondered if "they were preparing for some new ceremony. I imagined a huge sing with multiple bonfires. But my adult relatives were strangely quiet.

A week or two later the BIA workers returned and blocked one end of the trench they had dug, leaving the other end open. "You need to round up your sheep and goats," one man said, "and herd them into the trench." Grandfather started to protest but one of the BIA workers interrupted him, "Do not protest, Grandfather. He was using the polite form of address for a younger man addressing an elder. "Haven't you heard. You'll get thrown in jail?"

All but 300 of grandma's 1,000-head flock were herded into the trench. "Then the BIA workers sealed that end. A flammable material was sprayed on the animals, and they were set on fire. We couldn't believe what we were witnessing. I covered my ears, but could not block the shrieks of the animals, especially the goats, who had a high, piercing cry. The stench of burning wool and flesh filled the normally fresh air," Chester said. In just a short time, years of hard work and their life savings were gone.

We learned that any family with more than 100 sheep and goats was subject to the "reduction." The promises made, most of which never happened, had convinced enough Navajo people to approve the stock reduction referendums. The devastation they were now feeling had been approved by their own people.

They would not be fooled again. When it came time to vote on acceptance of John Collier's Indian Reorganization Act (IRA) the Navajo voted against it. John Collier blamed this on other things and other people, but the handwriting was on the wall.

Back in the 1860s, the Navajo people, my ancestors, lost all their wealth at the hands of the federal government's army under the direction of General James Carleton. Kit Carson executed the orders, and the army destroyed Navajo crops and homes, confiscated or killed their livestock as they themselves were rounded up and sent to be exiled at Bosque Redondo for four long years.

In 1868, the Navajo were sent to a new reservation located on their original homelands. This was accomplished by a treaty signed that same year. The Navajo had to start over again, but managed to build a life for themselves. Once again in the 1930s, the federal government came in and destroyed their wealth and livelihood.

CHAPTER 18

My Mom

Bessie Todecheenie

My Mom, Bessie Todecheenie (sometimes spelled Tudicheney), was born in about 1926 (or possibly 1931 or '32, if the 1950 census is correct) to Louise and Omar Todecheenie.

I would describe Mom as a kind, gentle woman, and a long-suffering wife. I remember her as having a quiet demeanor—she didn't socialize much except with family. She never spoke a mean word.

She attended both the Presbyterian Church in Cornfields, as well as often helping with the Navajo ceremonies and singing. While the worship and rituals were different, they worshiped the same God.

Mom was a good cook. Making doughnuts for the kids was her specialty. Everybody loved her cooking. I guess I was kind of a mama's girl. I remember having my hands in the flour and, to be honest probably all over myself, as she taught me how to make the dough and roll it in preparation for making frybread. I had fun doing things with Mom.

My big sister Jessie's dad died when she was very young. The timing is difficult for me to establish but my mom's relationship, which I described in the first paragraph of this book, with my biological dad must have been during the time between the death of Jessie's dad or perhaps her separation from him and Mom's marriage to my stepdad.

I was either very young or perhaps not yet born when Mom married my stepdad. To that marriage were born brothers Wilbert, Nelson, Martinez, Gilbert, Alfred and Kenneth and two sisters, Marilyn and Geneva. So, including Jessie and me, we had a family of ten children. Both my mom and my stepdad were hard workers. As a young woman, my mom worked for probably three years or more at the Navajo Ordnance Depot in Bellemont, AZ. My mom was one of a group of Navajo women who performed a very important roll readying the munitions in preparation for an anticipated invasion of Japan. This continued with the wars that followed, up to and including the Gulf War. To this day, the more I find out about it, the more proud I am of Mom.

My mom and stepdad.

After she married my stepdad, she worked through the chapter house clearing cactus from the grazing areas. My stepdad worked off the reservation on high power electricity transmission towers. Even with a very large family, we always seemed to have what we needed. While we were certainly not rich, I don't remember thinking we were poor and struggling like many others around us.

Mom provided a happy childhood for me, but I was always haunted by being different from the other kids. I always wondered why was I so light skinned when all the other kids were brown. When I asked Mom, she would just smile.

As I think back about my childhood, I often wonder if I was "spoiled" at home because I was different, but also picked on and bullied at school. I was always Mom's tag-along, following her like a shadow. When she worked at the chapter house, she would take me with her. I remember playing there while she was working in the fields.

I remember one time when another girl and I were hungry, and we peeked into the workers' lunch bags. We found a can of sardines, which we promptly opened and ate. We were discovered, and while we blamed each other, we were both at fault. I guess I deserved it when the sardines made me sick to my stomach. To this day I still have a dislike for sardines and I shy away from them..

Both Mom and Grandma wove rugs. Mom patiently taught me how to card wool and spin it into yarn. Then she helped me to weave a small child-sized rug. She was very patient.

If you search "Hubbell Rug" on the internet, you will learn that in the late 1920s or early 1930s Lorenzo Hubbell, one of John Lorenzo Hubbell's sons, commissioned Julia Joe to weave the largest existing Navajo rug in an effort to promote his trading post business in Winslow, AZ. In order to accommodate a loom of the size envisioned, Julia's husband, Sam, built an additional room onto their house.

The Hubbell Rug displayed in front of Hubbell's Trading Post.

Julia probably started weaving in 1932, and the rug was completed in 1937. Measuring 26 x 36 feet and weighing in excess of 250 pounds, the rug is made of the wool of 78 sheep—18 black and 60 white. This means a lot of carding, spinning and dying before the weaving could even begin.

What you probably won't learn in a computer search, is that Julia Joe was my grandma Louise's sister and that the daughters who helped their mom with the project are my aunts. Julia was a member of my family, my clan the Kinłichii'nii Clan or Red House People, sometimes referred to as the Rainbow clan. As with most things, my family worked together on projects, so I am sure Grandma Louise and probably Mom and Aunt Gladys (when they were old enough), helped with the massive job of carding and spinning of the wool.

As described earlier, when we were a little older, both Jessie and I spent a lot of time at Grandma's hogan or at school whenever my stepdad was home. When he was away working though, we lived with Mom. She had to know why Jessie and I spent so much time at Grandma's and why we wanted to go to Intermountain Indian School, but she didn't say much, if anything, about it. She wanted her children to have an education, so she supported our wishes.

Fond Memories

I remember planting corn with Mom, Grandma, and other relatives at Cornfields where we lived. It was hard work but fun doing things together.

After I came home from Intermountain Indian School and was old enough to drive, Mom bought a car. She did not drive, but now I could drive her places.

I remember one time when Mom and I went to Holbrook to shop. She liked a certain grocery store there, as well as a restaurant where we would go for lunch. While we were out, I asked her to buy me a six-pack of beer. At first, she refused but then relented. We were almost back to the reservation line when a policeman appeared behind us and turned on his red light.

I knew the police often stopped cars driven by Indians on their way back to the reservation. I guess they did this to make sure we weren't taking any prohibited things onto the reservation—like alcohol. Thinking about my six-pack of beer, I stepped on the gas and made it across the reservation line before the policeman could catch up with us.

As I looked in the rear-view mirror, I saw the police car turn around at the reservation border. Was this a recommended procedure? No. But I enjoyed my beer.

Mom and I had a special bond. I was the one who sat with her at the hospital for weeks at a time as she recovered from brain surgery. I was also the one who lived at her house so I could bring her home from the nursing home on weekends. I loved my mom and I always will.

Mom passed away in 1985, prematurely as a result of her health issues. Even in death, she was not done giving. As a result of me sitting with her following her brain surgery, the staff at St. Joseph's Hospital and I became familiar with one another and that gave me an advantage in getting hired as a nurses-aide there.

CHAPTER 19

My Dad

I was never given a chance to meet or know my dad, except when I was a baby. Mom obviously did not want to tell me that she'd had a relationship with a married man, until she was forced to do so. My Dad was about eighteen or nineteen years old when he and my Mom had their relationship.

My father, Jerald Mac Tanner, was born on March 7, 1934, in Farmington, San Juan County, New Mexico. He was the fifth child of Ruel Lehi Tanner and Stella McGee Tanner, who had eight children.

He met his death in the course of business when he chartered a single-engine plane, a Bonanza, in Gallup, New Mexico, to fly him to Battle Mountain, Nevada, to check on his turquoise mining operation. Former New Mexico Senator D. B. Clark, who was Dad's friend, was the pilot. They both died on impact when the plane crashed at night into Battle Mountain in Nevada on February 3, 1972. The crash site wasn't discovered for two days, so the deaths were recorded on either February 4th or 5th.

My cousin, Uncle Don's namesake son, wrote this memory for *Public Memory*:

Jerald Mac Tanner

"My Uncle Jerry died in a plane crash when I was a sophomore in high school. Sometime the next evening, my dad received a phone call from Jerry's wife, Tonis. She told him Jerry had not returned when expected and that she hadn't heard from him. Dad was a pilot and had his own twin-engine Cessna, so he decided to fly up and join the search.

The Civil Air Patrol had been notified and a search was to begin the next day. My cousin, Robert (Jerry's second son), and I – along with uncles J.B. "Buddy" and Joe Tanner, and Gallup's airport manager, Joe Danoff, flew to Battle Mountain with Dad, the next day.

On the second day of the search, someone in our plane spotted the single-engine plane we were looking for—on a mountain slope between Battle Mountain and Elko, Nevada. It was one of the strangest sites I've ever seen. There wasn't a scattering of wreckage that you'd typically expect to see. It looked like the airplane had just been placed there. I remember that it looked like the door was open on the passenger side.

We determined how to access the area, returned to Battle Mountain Airport and all (except me, Robert and Uncle Buddy) drove to the vicinity of the crash site. They were able to get within a half mile on a dirt road. Joe Danoff and Uncle Joe then hiked the remaining distance to the site. When they got to about a hundred feet away, Joe Danoff told Uncle Joe to wait while he went to check the plane. Both Jerry and Mr. Clark were dead – still strapped in their seats.

Joe Danoff and others speculated that they were flying after dark—parallel with the highway lights between Battle Mountain and Elko—and just "clipped" the top of an unseen ridge. The main power switch was in the "Off" position—indicating Clark knew they were going to crash-land and turned off all electricity to decrease the possibility of fire. The plane "pancaked" on the opposite slope—killing both instantly.

It was a sad and surreal experience.

In a footnote my cousin wrote,

> While we waited for news from the crash site, Uncle Buddy did his best to keep Robert (and me) distracted by putting coins in slot machines while we pulled the handles.

(The Robert that cousin Don wrote about is my half-brother, who was tragically killed in California by a drunk driver.)

Some Things I Learned about Dad

Dad was apparently an energetic young man on the road to becoming a successful businessman. He worked temporarily at a couple of other family-owned trading posts after he left Sunrise Trading Post, but was on his way to owning many different businesses.

His first, at twenty years old, was with a partner. They started a jukebox business that operated in three states for a couple of years. Tabletop jukeboxes were popular in the 1950s. They were smaller versions of regular jukeboxes that could be placed at each table or booth in diners so customers could play music while waiting for their orders. This meant they didn't need to leave their tables to select and listen to music.

Dad chose the bustling town of Kayenta, Arizona, to install the first of his line of these small jukeboxes in restaurants there, then added other establishments around northern Arizona and New Mexico and southern Colorado in the Four Corners area.

My Uncle chuckled as he remembered my Dad scurrying from place to place to collect his nickels, dimes and quarters. Perhaps Dad's favorite song was the catchy little tune written by Stephen Weiss and Bernie Baum and made popular in the '50s by Teresa Brewer, Petula Clark and other singers:

Tabletop jukeboxes were popular at this time.

"Music! Music! Music!" which encouraged listeners to put another nickel in the nickelodeon. But I am only guessing.

By the 1960s, Dad owned an Indian Gift Shop in Scottsdale, Arizona, that was located close to the intersection of Scottsdale Road and Main Street in what is now referred to as Old Town Scottsdale. During a recent visit with my brother and sister-in-law, my sister-in-law told me about being in an antique store and looking through old picture postcards in search of anything of interest.

One of the postcards flipped out of the box it was in and landed upside down on the floor next to her. When she picked it up and looked at it, it was a picture of Dad's store in Scottsdale. I can't help but wonder if it was Dad's spirit that flipped the postcard out of the box so it could appear in my book. I like to think so. Anyway, here it is.

I found out later that Dad had left the shop in Arizona suddenly and moved to Washington State, where his wife Pat's brother lived. He found work at Sears, and in only a few months became the manager of the Men's Department. A few years later, he left Washington and returned with his family to Gallup, New Mexico, where he started his own wholesale business selling Navajo rugs on the road. He traveled through five states doing this. Eventually, he added the work of other native artists and silversmiths, plus a leather belt manufacturing operation he started, all adding to the inventory of items he wholesaled to other businesses.

Dad also acquired an interest in a turquoise mine in Nevada, which would contribute to his untimely death. The newspaper that reported the plane crash that took his life wrote that Dad was the owner of the Jerry Tanner Trading Post near Zuni, New Mexico.

Before moving on to other ventures, Dad worked for my Anglo Grandma Stella's younger brother, Uncle Ellis McGee, at the Sunrise Trading Post in Sunrise. Grandma Stella Tanner's maiden name was McGee. He probably

Dad, on the right.

Dad at work.

Dad relaxing

worked there for two or three years during his late teens, and it was there and during this time that he and my mom became my parents.

Perhaps I'm feeling a bit nostalgic and deprived, but I wish I had known my dad. I wish I could have had an opportunity to hug him and to have told him at least once, "I love you, Daddy."

I often wonder how my childhood would have been if I had known my father and had a relationship with him. I also wonder now what was really going on behind my back. Did everybody know except me? I remember on more than one occasion going to Gallup with my aunt and visiting the stores that I now know my Tanner relatives owned. Was it just to get supplies for jewelry making or rug making? Did the store owners give me candy because they gave every child candy, or was I special to them? I guess I will never know.

Why I Decided to Learn About Dad

My delving into my Anglo family's existence and history started when one of my daughters, during her college years, started working on her family tree. I had known for a long time that my dad was Anglo, but that's about all I knew. One of my aunts though, knew about Dad's brothers, my uncles. With her help, my daughter and I started trying to put the family tree together, and the rest of my immediate family started getting interested.

As my first attempt at making contact with my Anglo family, I walked into Uncle Ellis Tanners' Trading Post in Gallup, New Mexico, and introduced myself as a family member. I remember I felt like my visit didn't go well and I was disappointed with how I was received. Afterwards, when I thought about it, I could understand why—he didn't know me and apparently what I said was a surprise to him.

My brother, Lynn, worked for Uncle Ellis at the time, but he was out for lunch when I popped in for my visit. Uncle Ellis, I was told later, called Lynn to tell him about our encounter. Lynn became interested and we talked by phone later that same day. We made arrangements to meet at

Native American Appreciation Day at Uncle Ellis Tanner's Trading Post.

my uncle's trading post, and this time the atmosphere was entirely different. We were now family.

Uncle Ellis, for over ten years, hosted a celebration of thanks at his trading post for all of his customers many of whom were Navajo. He called it Native American Appreciation Day. There would be lots of food and entertainment plus lots of prizes and give-a-ways, and just a fun time. Family members would attend and join in the merriment. I was shown a picture of my Anglo grandma, Grandma Stella, at her son's event. Although still able to walk she was being assisted in her wheelchair by a Navajo man

Me (Verna) visiting my Grandma Stella Tanner.

Me (Verna), daughter Manda, Grandma Stella, and daughter Harranna.

so she could make it around for the whole day, and just seeing the picture made me want to meet her.

My brother Lynn and I stayed in contact and we made arrangements to visit Grandma Stella at the Farmington, New Mexico retirement home where she lived. Grandma Stella was obviously thrilled with the idea of some of my family and I coming to visit her She said I reminded her of when she was my age. She wouldn't let go of my hand and continued to touch my face. The visit was so enjoyable, so memorable, that we visited her several times after the first.

When Grandma Stella passed away, some of my family and I went to the funeral. I was surprised to hear several of my grandma's family comment that I reminded them of grandma in her younger years. They said I was "an image of grandma." While it was a sad occasion, I was grateful I was able to attend the funeral. While we were there, my brother, Lynn, showed me the grave-sites of Dad, my Grandpa Ruel Lehi Tanner, and our younger brother, Robert Timothy Tanner.

My (Verna's) Tanner aunt and uncles, left to right: Uncle Rick, Uncle Don, my Dad Jerald, Aunt Dorothy, Uncle Joe, Grandma Stella, Uncle Bob, Uncle Ellis, and Uncle J.B. "Buddy".

Dad's gravesite.

CHAPTER 20

Japan's Deadly Mistake

In September 1939, Hitler's Germany invaded Poland, prompting Great Britain and France to declare war on Germany. The United States stayed out of the war until Pearl Harbor was bombed by the Japanese on December 7, 1941. The next day, the United States entered World War II.

After long discussions, President Roosevelt and Winston Churchill, Prime Minister of Great Britain, agreed that Hitler must be defeated in Europe first before turning to Japan. The United States switched to full wartime status, and while Japan was digging in and fortifying their islands in the Pacific (because of distance they would be necessary in any attack on Japan), the United States and its allies concentrated on defeating Germany and its allies.

On May 8, 1945, Germany surrendered and the United States could now turn its attention to defeating Japan. The battle plan was to first take control of the islands in the Pacific Ocean so they could be used as jumping-off points in an attack on the Japanese mainland. They would also be used for refueling stops and as a place to land disabled aircraft that could not make it back to home base.

They knew these islands were heavily fortified because they were just as important to Japan's defenses as they were to the anticipated attack on Japan by the United States. That being the case, Japan was clearly in a superior position, especially since they were experts at breaking any secret code used against them so far.

Philip Johnston, a civil engineer for the city of Los Angeles, had grown up on the Navajo Reservation because his parents had been missionaries to the Navajo. Johnston served in the military during World War I, and knew how important secret communication was in battle. Because he grew up on the Navajo Reservation, he was aware of how intricate and complex the Navajo language was and that it was almost impossible to master unless you learned it from birth. He came up with the idea to develop a code using the Navajo language and presented it to military officials. His plan was met with skepticism but they finally agreed to give it a try.

Even as early as 1940, the Navajo Tribal Council had made it known that the Navajo people were ready to help defend their country. They even passed a resolution that said,

> ...we resolve that the Navajo Indians stand ready, as they did in 1918, to aid and defend our Government and its institutions against all subversive and armed conflict and pledge our loyalty to the system which recognizes minority rights and a way of life that has placed us among the great people of our race.

Marine recruiters were sent to the boarding schools at Fort Defiance, Fort Wingate and Shiprock to recruit thirty Marines who spoke both Navajo and English. These recruits were told they would be working on a special project if they were chosen. Over 200 applied but only 30 were chosen. Of these, 29 were Marine recruits and on their way to boot camp outside of San Diego. There, they joined other recruits for the rigorous training Marines are known for. The thirtieth recruit dropped out so that he could play football during his senior year of high school. His intent was to rejoin the group after graduation, but he got hurt playing football and no longer qualified.

At the end of basic training, while the others in their class were given two weeks of leave, the 29 were finally told what their special project was.

Code talker recruits being sworn in. This picture hangs on the wall in the lobby of the National Archives in Riverside, CA.

These 29 men were charged with developing a secret code for transmitting messages during battle. These messages would not be in the Navajo language, but they would use Navajo words as code for other words. This combination is what made the Navajo code unbreakable, but it also meant those using the code had to memorize everything because nothing was written down so it could not be stolen by the enemy.

Once the code was completed and memorized, the 29 practiced, and practiced, and practiced. Finally, they were ready for test runs. All of this preparation had been necessary because they still had to convince the officials in charge that it would work and be faster than the old system.

They were still met with skepticism, but the tests proved that sending and receiving a message using the old system usually took up to four hours and the same message could be sent and received by the code talkers in less than four minutes.

When this new means of communication was first implemented, it was still so secret that the test messages that went out caused a panic because some thought what they were hearing on their radios was Japanese and that the Japanese had broken into their communication system. With the test run behind them, the 29 were ready to test their system in battle, so they were shipped out to Guadalcanal.

When they landed, they found themselves in a jungle. How could they fight an enemy that they could not see? Their only contact with their command was the radios. For the code talkers, there was no time to be scared—they had a job to do and it had to be perfect or fellow Marines would die.

The code talker system functioned admirably, and eventually the Japanese were forced to abandon Guadalcanal. Major General Alexander Vandegrift, leader of the Guadalcanal expedition, requested 83 more code talkers after seeing the success first hand.

The next stop for the code talkers was Rabaul, where they helped turn the tide. Their help in the Solomon Islands also secured that area and stalled the Japanese momentum. Unfortunately, with their advancement stopped, the Japanese dug their heels in on the other islands.

The code talkers had proven themselves over and over, and now moved on to the Gilbert Islands, with Tarawa being first. The Japanese were waiting for them there in small machine gun pill-boxes, and even intense bombing raids did not rid the island of the strong Japanese presence. The coral reefs in the area made approaching the island's beaches difficult, so the Marines were forced to wade ashore as the Japanese machine guns blazed. The code talkers were invaluable in coordinating the attack and minimizing death due to friendly fire. Even with this added help, it took four days to secure the island, and 1000 of the 16,000 attackers were killed and about 2,000 injured.

The death toll in this campaign was large, but they were learning how to be more effective and were making progress. Their next stop was the Marshall Islands where success came easier.

Next came Saipan, where 31,000 Japanese fighters were waiting in caves and on rugged slopes. After three weeks of fighting, the code talkers and the men they were fighting with were victorious. Tinian was taken relatively easy as well. Little did the Japanese know they were up against the code talkers who were coordinating the attacks making them much more effective.

Their third stop in the Mariana Island string was Guam, where the code talkers were invaluable. By this point, everyone in the military saw how important the code talkers were to winning the war.

While the fighting was going on and being coordinated through the code talkers' secret messages, bulldozers were busy making runways on the Mariana Islands. They were creating airstrips where the B-29s could take off to make the 3,000-mile round trip to bombing targets in Tokyo and other Japanese cities.

While the fighting had been intense and the death toll was mounting, the worst was yet to come. Iwo Jima, located halfway between the Mariana Islands and Tokyo, was where three important Japanese air strips were located. Iwo Jima is a miserable rugged stone projection jutting up from the ocean. It has essentially no vegetation, no drinkable water and sulfur laden air. It is five miles long and only about two and a half miles wide at its widest point. This miserable place was immensely important to both Japan and the United States. Japan needed it if they were to be successful in defending their island nation, and the United States needed it to be close enough to attack Japan and win the war.

Because of it's strategic location, Japan had 22,000 troops in place on the island ready to defend it. There was no good place to land a fighting force on Iwo Jima—one shore had an easier approach but the pounding surf would tear landing craft apart, the other shore had calmer waters but a terrible beach that sloped steeply upward. The U.S. chose the calmer side, but first bomber crews bombed the island for 74 consecutive days.

In preparation for the impending attack, 8,000 volleys of shelling peppered the beaches and hills of Iwo Jima. At 8:30 in the morning, 1,400 Marines were ready to deploy. They made it to the beach with very little resistance. When the beach was crowded with Marines, the Japanese soldiers opened fire. The code talkers were faced with digging a makeshift foxhole and setting up their radios as bullets whizzed past their heads and mortar shells landed nearby. But set it up they did and they went straight to work.

It was in this campaign that the code talkers would shine their brightest. Under the worst of working conditions, they remembered their code perfectly. They relayed the messages that coordinated the battle and this resulted in victory after about a month of intense fighting.

The Battle of Iwo Jima claimed the lives of 6,800 United States servicemen, and another 20,000 were wounded. Japan, however, lost nearly all of the 22,000 soldiers stationed there. Major Howard Conner, signal officer of the Fifth Marine Division, is quoted as saying, "Were it not for the Navajo code talkers, the Marines never would have taken Iwo Jima."

The code talkers' work was not yet done. Next, they moved on to Okinawa, located less than 400 miles from Japan. They would fight for over two months here, and lose more men than they had at Iwo Jima before victory was theirs.

Finally, they were ready to invade Japan itself. As they waited for orders, the *Enola Gay* took off from the island of Tinian where they had fought weeks ago. The story is told that as they waited for orders in Okinawa, the Navajo code talker who was manning the radio received a message. "Instantly he leaped to his feet and started dancing. Pounding out a rhythm as he danced, he made his way to the officer's tents. There, he broke the news that, following the atomic bomb blasts destroying Hiroshima and Nagasaki, Japan had surrendered."

The war was over. They would be going home.

Grandma didn't tell us about the Navajo code talkers because she didn't know about them. The code talkers were sworn to secrecy so that the system could be used for future wars if necessary. It was used again, to a much smaller extent, in the Korean and Vietnam campaigns. It was hard for these returning Marines to keep this information to themselves. They couldn't even tell their families what they did during the war as a Marine. Finally, the Navajo secret code was declassified in 1968 and the Navajo could at last be recognized for the part they played in winning World War II.

In 1982, President Ronald Reagan was the first to officially recognize the contribution the code talkers had made by giving them a certificate of recognition and declaring August 14 to be National Code Talkers Day. Then, in December 2000, President Bill Clinton signed a bill passed by Congress that recognized the Navajo code talkers and authorized awarding gold medals to the original 29 and silver medals to the rest. Only four of the original 29 were able to make the trip to Washington, D.C., where President George W. Bush presented them with their gold medals on July 26, 2001.

***

In researching for this chapter I came upon a story in Chester Nez's book, *Code Talker*, that made me smile. The rations provided by the military did not include frybread and the Navajo missed their frybread. So, using one of their helmets as a fry pan, they scooped in some lard and heated it on a butane heater. While it was getting hot, they mixed some flour and baking powder (if they had any) with water and made a ball of dough. Then they flatted the dough and fried it in the helmet. As they were camped in the jungles on some remote island, this tasted like home.

The *Fuji Evening*, a Tokyo newspaper wrote: "If the Japanese Imperial Intelligence Team could have decoded the Navajo messages … the history of the Pacific War might have turned out completely different."

As I was writing this chapter, this thought kept entering my head, *It's rather ironic, isn't it, that after years of effort on the part of the federal government boarding schools to get rid of the Navajo language and make these students into "white" kids, those young Navajos won the war against Japan because the boarding schools failed in their effort to do just that.*

The War Effort at Home

As important as the code talkers were, there is another story that needs to be told. In 1942, as part of the war effort back home, ordnance depots sprung up, one of which was the Navajo Ordnance Depot at Bellemont, Arizona, located about eleven miles west of Flagstaff. Their purpose was

Igloo for storage of munitions at Navajo Ordnance Depot.

a storage place for the munitions of war that would be needed in the war in the Pacific. Concrete bunkers that they called igloos were constructed for storing things like bombs until they were needed. Railroad spurs were constructed to bring the boxcars full of munitions to the depot. Once the depot was constructed and ready to function there was a great need for workers.

At this time Flagstaff consisted mostly of the homes of timber workers. Arizona State Teachers College, which would become Northern Arizona University, was there but it was struggling. The Depression had taken its toll there as it had all over the country.

The advent of the war would transform Flagstaff from a struggling small town into a dynamic city, first by the influx of workers for the ordnance depot, mostly by luring the Navajo and Hopi people off of the reservation to assume jobs at the depot, but also because the Navy established a training center at the college for young men entering the Navy. (I found it interesting in doing the research for this chapter to learn that Robert (Bobby) Kennedy was one of the Naval recruits trained there. One of my uncles also got his Naval recruit training there.)

The Navajo, my ancestors, were in dire need of employment, as was most everyone else in the country at that time. During the Depression, there were few jobs on the Reservation and the livestock reduction program had robbed many of the people of their wealth. The Navajo people, like the people in the rest of the country, were feeling the effects of the Great Depression that had started in 1929. Jobs were hard to find.

In the beginning, the depot needed strong men who could handle heavy bombs, but most of the men of military age were off serving their country or soon would be. By late 1942, the depot needed 2,000 workers, but they were only able to find 915. That is when they turned to the Navajo and Hopi. Mostly Navajo workers were used to unload boxcars of ammunition into trucks that would haul the load to the igloos where the boxes would be unloaded and stacked in the igloos. In January 1944 alone, 493 boxcars of ammunition arrived at the depot, and 334 boxcars were reloaded and shipped out. The workload was massive.

The Navajo were good workers but they had no place to live while they were there. At first, they built shanties—temporary shelters—along the road or in the forest a ways from the depot. The Major in charge saw what was happening and solved the problem by building housing on the base. The first try was only partially successful— the Hopis were okay with tents but the Navajo wanted hogans. When they finally constructed hogans, the Indian village was more stable. Indians made up 60 percent of the workforce, so they deserved the attention of those in charge.

Even with housing, life was not easy here for the Indians and many gave up and went back to the Reservation. Getting from place to place was difficult, since all they could do was walk. Liquor salesmen were always tempting them, language was a problem in getting needed supplies and many stores wouldn't cash their paychecks.

Again, the officers in charge saw that their workers weren't eating good diets and they were getting tired easily. They solved that problem by convincing Richardson and Young, Indian traders, to open a trading post at the depot. So, the Richardson Trading Post was built and Billy Young managed it. This made life easier and more normal for the Navajo and Hopi.

Billy Young, a true old-time trader, deserves a lot of credit for the success of the Navajo and Hopi workforce at the depot. He provided food for destitute families, gave credit to newcomers until they got their first paycheck, and donated candy, fruit and nuts for Christmas stockings for the village children. He also donated prizes for the Indian Field Day events and sweaters for the baby contest winners. He would often even pay the fine for young Indians who had gotten arrested on Saturday night after drinking too much. He not only knew they would repay him but he knew the depot needed the work force for the war effort. Billy Young made the depot a happy place to work. (Lambing season was still a problem and caused major absenteeism though.)

In January of 1943, Lieutenant McGee was assigned to uncover problems with the Indian workforce. He discovered that Anglo and Hispanic women were employed at the depot but Indian women were not. By February 1943, 290 Indian women had been hired. They now made up 14 percent of the workforce, and before long the percentage would double.

I have not been able to uncover much information, but I know that my mother worked at the depot in Bellemont. When and for how long I do not know, but circumstances would suggest that she was probably one of the 290 in 1943. They were called "women ordnance workers" or "WOWs" for short.

In his book *Arizona's War Town,* John S. Westerlund writes about the female workforce, saying that in 1943 the ordnance department publicized a survey reflecting attitudes of the period. The survey said that women had greater finger dexterity than men, greater patience than men, greater enthusiasm than men, they took instruction far more personally, that they were more patriotic, that they did not mind getting their hands and face dirty but they wanted beauty shops available.

As the war effort wound down, the Navajo Ordnance Depot was chosen to stay open while others were closed. The ammunition stored there was in readiness for the invasion of Japan that did not happen. The ammunition stayed there for 50 years before it was destroyed as it became unserviceable.

In 1993 the ownership of the depot was transferred to Arizona and it is currently the home of the Arizona National Guard.

Sixty-nine hogans were built to house Navajo workers.

A typica; hogan at Navajo Ordnance Depot.

Sweat Lodge at Navajo Ordnance Depot.

Tents for workers at Navajo Ordnance Depot.

Women workers at Navajo
Ordnance Depot.

I was originally sure the Navajo lady on the left in the top right photo was Mom, but the dates on the picture and the 1950 census records do not coordinate, so maybe not.

CHAPTER 21

My Professional Career: Memorable Patients

G randma Louise Todecheenie was a talented midwife. She was willing to help expectant mothers near and far when her help was sought, day or night. I spent a lot of time with Grandma and that is probably why I chose the medical profession as my life's work. I loved my grandma.

When I finished high school, I enrolled in the nurses aide course at College of Ganado. Had the Nursing School still been in existence, I probably would have become a nurse, but it closed about the same year I was born. Only a few years later, the Presbyterian Church pretty much abandoned the Mission and turned it over to Project H.O.P.E., an international health care organization. So, while I am not certain, it was probably Project H.O.P.E. that ran the nurses aid training at the time I was enrolled there. At this same time, Project H.O.P.E was helping the Navajo tribe set up their own health care system.

Mom and my stepdad had moved off the Reservation to Parker, Arizona, for his work in field irrigation. Soon after, my husband, the kiddies and I moved to Parker too. My husband got a job as a heavy equipment operator. I loved that I was able to see Mom anytime I wanted and stay home with my children, but I wanted to get a job and put my education into practice.

My first job was in the cafeteria at the local school. It was there that I was required to change my hair style from long to short. I still wanted to work in the medical field, so I applied for a job as a nurses aid at Parker Community Hospital. I was interviewed and hired. I got a week of training, and for about three years I would float from unit to unit in the hospital, going wherever I was needed. That was my entry into my chosen profession and on a professional level, life was pretty good.

As years went by the requirements for my profession changed and I added to my education by becoming a Certified Nursing Assistant (CNA) and a Patient Care Technician (PCT).

Some years later, after we had established our home in Phoenix, I was working evenings as a nurses aide at St. Joseph's Hospital. I also enrolled in the data processing course at Mountain States Technical Institute and graduated with an Associate's Degree in Data Processing.

I worked at St. Joseph's Hospital for about 10 years. I had a growing family to support and had never gotten any child support from my ex-husband. I determined that I could make more money by working through an agency, where I would be sent to various hospitals as they had a need for

Left, me (Verna) in cap and gown at graduation from Mountain States Technical Institute (photo embellished by one of my children).
Right, President's Honor List certificate.

an additional staff member. At one time or another, I worked at almost every hospital in the Phoenix area. Sometimes, I would be assigned to a private duty patient and would care for the patient in their home.

Some patients I had the opportunity to help with their recovery from surgery, others I helped as they battled disease or lived out their final years. Some were thoroughly enjoyable and others were not.

Perhaps the worst assignments, at least for me, were the newborns who had been brought into this world by mothers who were addicted to drugs. I loved working with babies, but trying to care for a newborn who was struggling with drug withdrawal broke my heart.

One child that I fondly and broken heartedly remember was a little girl who had been transferred to the hospital where I worked for care. She had experienced brutal sexual abuse and needed to be loved but didn't know who she could trust. For whatever reason, she took a liking to me. She trusted me and wanted no one else on the staff except me to attend to her needs. While I was happy to be her trusted friend, I had to go home to my own family at the end of my shift each day. It broke my heart to have to leave her as she cried for me to stay.

I thoroughly enjoyed most of my jobs, though the staff members at one hospital were a little bit crazy. They were convinced the hospital was haunted by the spirits of previous patients. Maybe they were just trying to scare me? They talked about hearing doors mysteriously opening and closing when no one was near, about shadows moving in the hallways and feeling unexplained cold drafts. Maybe I once saw a shadow and once felt a cold draft. Was I coming under their spell? That job was spooky.

One incident that I remember was this huge lady, maybe my fattest patient ever. She went into Code Blue, meaning her heart had stopped. I tried, but there was no way I could do chest compressions because she was just too large. So, into the bed I jumped, and by straddling her body I was able to do effective chest compressions and we saved her life.

All was well until I went to the break room and had to face what my fellow workers were saying. "Verna jumped right in bed with the patient," they teased. "Verna was right on top of the patient." It was all in fun, and the outcome made the teasing fun for me too.

On another occasion, the Code Blue signal came for a patient who was on a ventilator. A nurse started down the hall with the Code Blue cart but I thought she was moving way too slowly. I was running toward the patient's room and I grabbed the cart, perhaps a little too violently, and raced down the hall. As I turned into the patient's room, I glanced back only to see the nurse getting up off the floor. I was sorry I had caused her to fall and I apologized, but I was happy that I got to the room in time to save the patient's life.

I remember an incident at one hospital when I was assigned to a Navajo man who was a heavy drinker and was suffering from kidney failure. He was amazed when I spoke to him in the Navajo language. "I thought you were a white lady," he said.

His family was in the process of testing family members for compatibility, because the only thing the doctors said would save my patient was a kidney transplant. One family member turned out to be a match, but their kidneys were also about to fail due to drinking.

When I came to work that day, my patient was in a jovial mood. He said, "Yeah, my brother is a match, but he drank too much too, and his kidneys are jacked up worse than mine." As soon as I came on duty the following day, I went to check on my patient, but sadly he had passed away the night before.

One private duty couple that I cared for sticks in my mind because of an incident that happened while I was there. I had helped to care for the elderly couple who lived in a pretty rural area on the south side of Phoenix, and after the husband passed away I continued helping to care for the widow, Bessie (not her real name).

Their housekeeper had warned me that mice and snakes were frequent visitors to the home. One day when I was there, all of a sudden we heard a plop. A snake of some considerable size, had managed to squeeze through the opening in a vent high up on the wall without us noticing, and the noise we heard was it falling to the floor. I grabbed a plastic storage container and trapped the snake so we could call city animal control to come and rescue it. Well, really it was to rescue us, since as I mentioned earlier, I have no love for snakes.

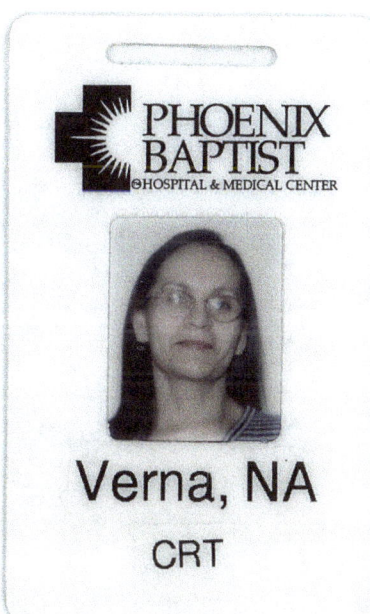

Verna Begay CNA

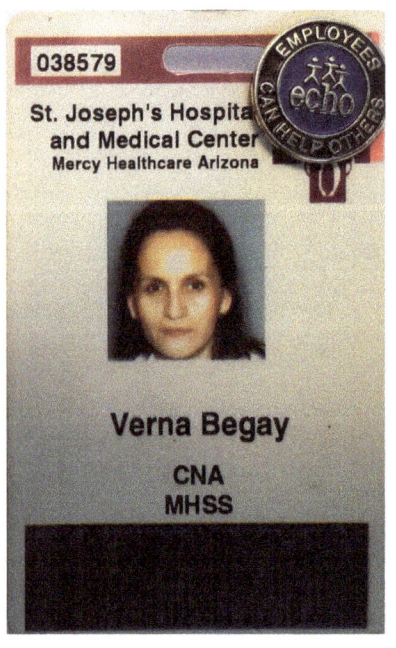

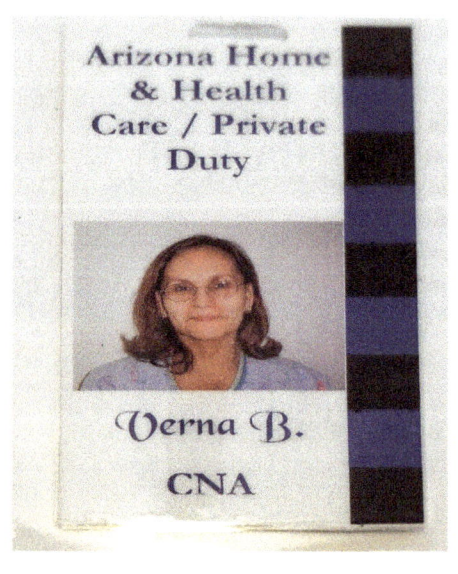

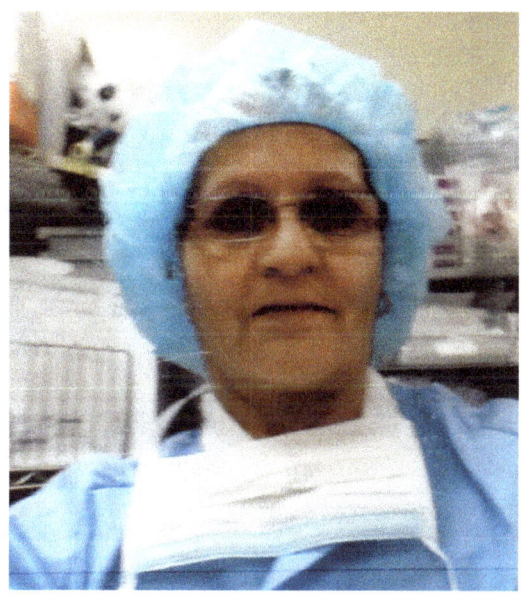

*Me (Verna) on lunch break at Mayo
Hospital.*

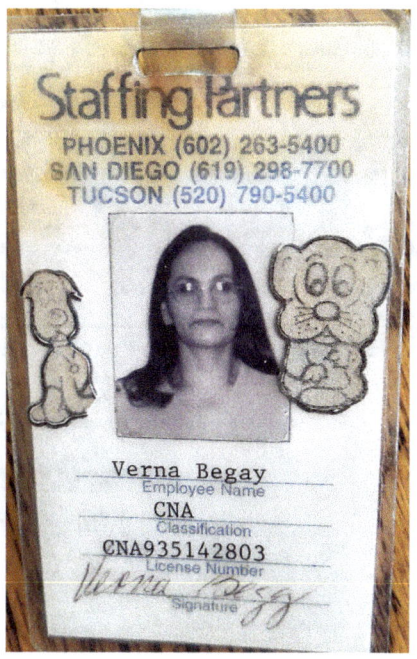

Caring for my patient in Minnesota. Patient on left, me in center, my husband on the right.

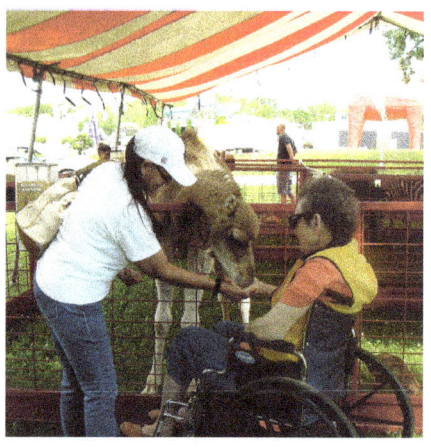

Me helping my patient feed a young camel at a county fair.

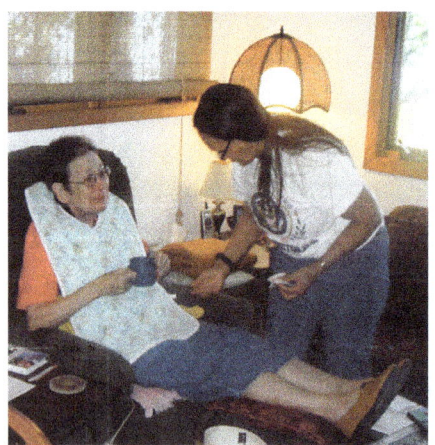

My patient and me at her home.

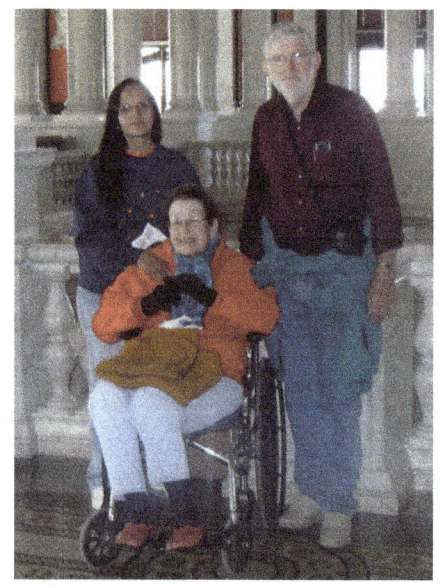

My patient, her husband and me at the Library of Congress.

Another private duty patient I cared for I only remember as Mr. Alexander (not his real name). He was a principal figure in a bank, the name of which I have forgotten. I was interviewed by his family, approved, and then went to work in their absolutely beautiful home.

One of my patients and me at the St. Paul Cathedral in St. Paul, Minnesota.

Mr. Alexander loved eating oysters and caviar, neither of which looked very appealing to me. "Try some," he would say, "they are delicious. You will like it." But the sound that he made as I helped him to eat the oysters was enough to convince me that I would save all the oysters for him. It's a sound that I will never forget.

A United States Senator was one of Mr. Alexander's friends and he would come to visit. I had met the Senator as a customer at the Hubbell Trading Post, but his visits with Mr. Alexander

My patient on left, me in the center and my husband on the right at Bullfeathers in Washington, D.C.

were in an entirely different setting, which made it seem different. Even though he was there to visit Mr. Alexander, I felt like I got to know him on a more personal level.

This is also where I had the opportunity to meet K.J. who played for the Phoenix Suns professional basketball team. That was a thrill because ever since playing for the Greasewood Boarding School Mustangs, I have been a fan of basketball. I guess he wasn't the tallest member of the Suns team, but wow was he tall. K.J. had come to visit Mr. Alexander but he still took time to give me his autograph.

It was probably because of Mr. Alexander's influence that I was hired to assist the Senator's mother until she deteriorated to the point that she needed 24-hour care, for which I was not licensed. Later, when the Senator himself needed nursing care, I was contacted. Unfortunately, he needed 24-hour care which I could not provide. I vividly remember the beautiful Navajo rugs the Senator had in his home. His collection of Indian artifacts and rugs was extensive, which made his home a very pleasant place to work.

In addition to sometimes working in extraordinary homes, I would also have to look the other way to allow the residents of the home some privacy. My patient, Laura (not her real name), was from California and a nurse herself. She was staying with her sister, and that is where I was hired to assist her.

My story isn't about this patient though, it's about her wealthy but eccentric sister. I say wealthy because she drove a Jaguar, an expensive car, and had another expensive car, a Rolls Royce, in the garage. She also had an extraordinary house. This is how I got to ride in a Rolls Royce! We drove it to take my patient to an appointment.

One day when the sister had a gentleman visitor, they disappeared into her room and closed the door. I don't remember the details, but I needed to get the sister's attention for something my patient needed right away. I knocked on her door, and out came the sister with her pants on backwards! I did a double take, but said nothing. My patient's needs were satisfied and the sister went back into her room.

Later, the sister apologized for the incident. I was asked if I would travel to California with them and I consented, but sadly my patient passed away before that trip happened.

Travel was also a part of the nursing service I was hired to do for some patients. I was hired by a woman who owned an agency that sent traveling nurses on assignments throughout the world to assist patients with respiratory problems. She had an agency in Phoenix that sent nurses wherever they were needed. I would travel with her and her dad, my patient, back and forth between Phoenix and Texas where they lived. I remember they always ate Morning Star bacon and sausage, and I guess I developed a liking for it because I still eat it from time to time.

Most of my private duty patients were from wealthy families and most of them started treating me like family after a while. So, it was extra sad when my patient would pass on.

One very memorable patient was a biker who was a member of a biker gang. All of the nursing assistants at the Agency were afraid to go to his house. "I'm not afraid to take care of him," I said. "How dangerous can he be? He's on full oxygen and attached to a large oxygen tank."

In the beginning, he tried to be aggressive with me, but he soon realized that I would not be scared off. Besides, he needed help. Little by little, I got him to cooperate so I could administer good care. His wife, who was quite a bit younger than him, worked a lot of hours at a restaurant, so much of the time it was just him and me.

He finally allowed me to comb his long hair and braid it. His wife was amazed that he let me do that for him. While I worked, he would tell me stories about how, as a teenager, he got involved in gangs and how he killed a person at a grocery store when he was just a teenager. He said he had to kill in order to survive.

He also told me he never went anywhere without his switchblade and gun. His other stories included how he robbed a grocery store and about a shoot-out that he was a part of. For quite some time he continued to tell me things like this to try to scare me, but I wouldn't scare so he finally pretty much gave up.

He told me how he used to drink a lot, and I suspect he probably still did some. Also, how he smoked marijuana and did drugs. He couldn't smoke anymore, with the oxygen therapy, but he still chewed tobacco.

It was a challenge convincing him that he needed to take a bath. I remember sparring verbally over whether he would allow me to soak his feet. "Your feet are stinky," I said.

Of course, his reply was, "My feet do not stink!" Eventually I prevailed.

He was very protective of the jacket that designated his gang. He would not allow anyone to touch it, but eventually he offered to let me put it on. I don't think he was able to be close friends with anyone but his biker buddies, but he couldn't scare me so I think that translated into some friendly affection. He even allowed me to sit on his motorcycle.

He told me about how his gang would get in gang wars with an enemy gang that often resulted in death on both sides. On his birthday, he asked me to take him to a party at another biker's house (maybe gang headquarters?). It turned out the party was at a house that had been made bullet-proof—even the windows were made of bullet-proof glass.

Inside, the house was set up like a bar, with pool tables and a well-furnished bar. The walls and even the ceiling were covered with license plates from states all over the country. I wondered how they acquired those, but wisely decided not to ask.

One time in relating that story to some of my family, my son-in-law, who is also a biker, said to me, "I don't believe you actually had the courage to go into that house."

"I was not afraid," I said, "as long as I was with my patient." He was writing a book about his life and he promised me a copy when it was finished. I'm not sure if he had the book finished when he passed away but I am still waiting for my copy.

My time assisting a patient at a facility designed to give residents with memory loss a pleasant place to spend their remaining years was especially emotional. My patient there was the husband of a well-known attorney of considerable status in the legal world. On this particular weekend, the facility had organized a cookout for the residents so family members could come and have a meal with their loved ones.

My patient and a lady resident of the facility had developed a relationship, as so often happens with dementia patients who can no longer remember their spouses or families. On this particular occasion, I was helping to serve food to the residents and their guests when my patients "girlfriend" showed up and was making a scene because someone else was with her "boyfriend." We had to gently remove her from the area so the attorney and her husband could eat their meal unmolested. This was a sad but humorous incident.

The other happening I remember vividly was just plain sad and made me emotional. A Navajo man was jaywalking across the street when he was hit and killed by a car driven by a certain priest whose name I will keep private. The Navajo man who was killed was a good friend of my husband, Manley, and I.

Yes, he drank too much sometimes and that is most likely what caused him to be jaywalking that night. But, that did not excuse the driver who left the scene of the accident. The priest faced the judge, not on a charge of murder, but a charge of hit and run. We all thought the judge went easy on him with the sentence he handed down. The court had spoken, but when that same priest showed up to minister to the residents of the facility where I was working, I confronted the authorities about allowing this dishonorable priest to minister there.

There were also the "almost" scrapes with fame. A very famous singer and actor (whose name I am prohibited from stating because of HIPA rules) was aging and he was in need of nursing care. His family had applied to the agency for which I worked asking for a nursing assistant. So, I applied for the job. I passed the background study, had the personal interview and had been approved when they decided that what they needed was an around the clock nurse instead. I was not qualified for the position with that requirement.

Then there was the application by a couple, who are famous movie stars (again I cannot name them because of HIPA rules), asking for a nursing assistant to help with their children. I passed the background study here as well, sat for the interview and was approved for the job. I was all set to go, but I wanted my common law husband to accompany me. They approved this but said he would have to pass a background study too. When they did the background study on my husband, there were things there they did not approve of. I sometimes second guess myself for making the decision not to accept the job because he couldn't accompany me.

My last private duty patient was a snowbird from Minnesota, who with her husband, spent winters at a retirement park where they owned a park model. After my first day, I almost decided not to go back. It had taken me over an hour to get to the job site, first walking to where the light rail stopped and then at the end of the light rail line transferring to a city bus. Thank goodness there was a bus stop at the entrance to the retirement park.

When I entered the park, I had no idea where to go. There were almost 2,000 park models to choose from. I called and her husband came and picked me up by the gate. In the evening I had to walk to the end of the block and cross the street in order to board the bus going the right way. Then there was another hour on the bus and light rail and then a walk to my home.

My patient, who had lung cancer, was such a sweet lady who was always smiling, and I enjoyed being with her and doing what I could to make life comfortable for her, so I continued and did so each winter for three or four years.

One incident that I remember was when I was walking to the bus stop one evening. As I crossed the street, a helicopter was circling the area. All of a sudden, someone in the helicopter shouted through a loud speaker, "Lady, get down! Get down! Take cover!" It took me a minute to realize they were talking to me. Apparently, there was a person with a gun they were tracking in the area. After my heart stopped racing, I boarded the bus.

One summer, I was hired to travel to Minnesota, along with my husband Manley, to take care of my patient for six weeks while her husband was doing volunteer work with an organization he belonged to. This was a welcome respite from the Phoenix heat.

On another occasion, I was hired to accompany my patient and her husband on a trip to Washington, D.C., to attend an educational conference. My husband and I flew to Minnesota and accompanied my patient and her husband to the conference. During free periods, we got to visit the Library of Congress and the United States Capitol, as well as the Washington Monument, the Lincoln Memorial and other sites around the city. It has been 12 years now since this patient passed away, but her husband and I have remained family and he is the co-author of my book.

My last agency job was as a fill-in setting up surgical suites at the Phoenix Mayo Hospital. My supervisor apparently approved of my work and would request that I be sent when the position needed to be filled. As time went on, he made it known to me that the position was going to become full-time and he would recommend that I be given the position because he liked the quality of my work.

The day before someone was to be chosen for the position, the hospital was holding an orientation session that he recommended I attend. I went to the orientation and waited the next few days for a phone call. None came. I found out when I inquired that the position had been filled internally. That hurt after I had been led to believe I would most likely get it. I never went back there to get my comfortable shoes from my locker. Oh well, they had some barbeque stains on them anyway.

CHAPTER 22

Grandma's Navajo Frybread

My career path then made a dramatic change in direction. We had a food trailer built that we designed to be a Navajo frybread kitchen. With the help of a graphic designer, my daughters Manda (Milo) and Mandy designed the exterior artwork on the trailer. After impatiently waiting for the trailer to be finished, it was finally ready for us to pick up. Then began the trying chore of getting all the permits and licenses required for food trailers—not an easy task for a newcomer.

For about seven years we operated the food trailer and developed a loyal following that would make it a point of attending any festival we happened to be a part of. We made Navajo frybread with powdered sugar and cinnamon, Navajo taco, Navajo burger and Navajo pork chops at Grandma's Navajo Frybread. Each dish was an adaptation of frybread. I loved seeing people line up to buy my food. Most festivals we were a part of were fun, though I usually hurt the next day.

Gassing up pulling our Grandma's Navajo Frybread trailer.

Golden brown frybread

Blue Bird flour makes the best frybread.

Chili beans ready to serve.

Customers lined up to buy from Grandma's Najavo Frybread.

A few festivals were harrowing or just plain disappointing though. I remember heading home after dark from one festival when all of a sudden I heard a loud bang and the truck became difficult to control. We had blown a tire on the food trailer. I'd had experience in earlier years towing a horse trailer to rodeos with my friends, so I guess I unconsciously did the right thing and prevented the trailer and truck from jackknifing.

We had a spare tire but did not have a jack capable of jacking up a multi-ton trailer. To make things worse, we were in a construction zone. The police were no help with finding someone with the proper equipment needed to change the tire. They just reminded us that we had to get moved out of the construction zone, immediately.

After several phone calls, we finally found a towing company that could do the job. They got the tire changed and we were on our way—at least two hours behind schedule.

Another disaster, at least business-wise, was a festival some 200 miles from home base. We got there the day before the festival was to start, and got set up and prepared for the next day. Overnight, a storm blew in rain and a cold blustery wind that lasted the entire weekend. Obviously, there were no customers coming out in that weather. Finally, the festival organizer came around to each of us vendors and told us we were free to leave.

We could count the number of frybreads we'd sold on one hand and have fingers left over. What was worse was that we had to drive 200 miles home and then dump all the prepared food in the garbage.

While that festival was painful for the bank account, there were two others that were painful in a different way. The first was a small event that I didn't expect to be very busy, so I only had a crew of two. While I was working, I guess I got in a hurry and did not lower the dough into the hot oil properly. Hot oil splashed onto my finger and it hurt like crazy. I foolishly put on a pair of rubber gloves and completed the order in progress.

Then I went off to Mayo Hospital, which was the closest emergency room to where our food truck was located. After the blistered skin was removed, my finger was bandaged and I went home to let it heal.

While burns are perhaps one of the most painful injuries, I tested that theory a year or so later. We arrived at the event the afternoon before it was to start and parked in a parking lot until I could find out where we were to set up. Instead of walking an extra block or so where I could have stayed on the hard surface, I decided to save some steps and walk through a shallow ditch from the parking lot to the hard surface.

Unfortunately, I slid on loose gravel, and fell. When I looked at my foot, it was at a right angle to my leg. There was no way I could stand up. My husband and another man who happened to see my predicament had to carry me to the truck, and again we were off to the closest emergency room which was Mayo Hospital again. I had to get my seriously broken ankle stabilized. Obviously we were a no-show at the event that weekend.

We had another event scheduled a week later, so my kids filled in and did a marvelous job making frybread.

A few days later, I was off to Mayo again for x-rays which resulted in a recommendation that surgery was needed to insert a bone plate and several pins. Doing this would give me the best chance of a normal ankle after it healed.

Navajo chili dog.

After two surgeries, one to put the bone place and pins in, and another to remove them after the ankle was healed, I now have a normal ankle.

Running a food truck was hard work but it was fun. We were a part of Superbowl 49's Fanfest in Scottsdale. We also

Breakfast sandwich served at Super Bowl 49.

Manley in a quiet moment.

My (Verna's) son, Harry, at the frybread trailer grill.

were at the Arizona National Livestock show between Christmas and New Years, the Dragon Boat Festival on Tempe Lake, the Native American Festival in Litchfield Park and the Labor Day weekend rodeo at the Santa Cruz County fairgrounds near Sonoita.

On two occasions we ventured out of Arizona to a car show in Needles, California, and to a music festival in Las Vegas, Nevada. Most of our festivals were in Arizona though. We were at the Tubac Art Festival in Tubac, the Superstition Mountain Museum Native American Festival, the Balloon Festival and others at Salt River Fields, the July 4th week rodeo in Prescott, Glendale Glitters in Glendale at Christmas time, the Buckeye Air Fair, the Northern Gila County Fair, the Lantern Festival at the Pinal County fairgrounds and several Magic Bird Art festivals in Cave Creek, Carefree and Fountain Hills.

In 2020, the Covid pandemic eliminated the large gatherings upon which our business depended. The state of Arizona gave us an opportunity to set up at highway rest stops, and we did a few of those. But it was decision time. Partly because of the Covid shutdown of business but also due to the toll working with the dough was having on my body, we made the difficult decision to end our food truck business Perhaps because I insisted on making the dough, rolling it, forming the frybread and frying it the traditional way, and even though my sister, Marilyn, often helped me make the dough, I was spending too much time hurting. I have to admit that while I had a mechanical dough maker, I seldom used it.

It was sad but Grandma's Navajo Frybread would be no more. It was time to retire; time to sit on the swing on the front porch and remember. My life has been a hard life at times, but it has been a good life and it still is.

Left to right: My daughter Angela, sister Marilyn and Me (Verna).

Three years later, I still get calls asking for my frybread. It makes me proud that people loved my frybread, which is also part of my heritage. I had so much fun running my frybread food trailer, with help from my children, my granddaughters, my sister, Marilyn and my husband, Manley. It was fun traveling to events throughout the state too.

Balloon Festival at Pinal County Fairgrounds.

I still make frybread for my family, especially when one of my grandchildren begs grandma for some. I hope future generations will not lose the frybread tradition.

Dragon Boat Festival on Tempe Town Lake.

Super Bowl 49.

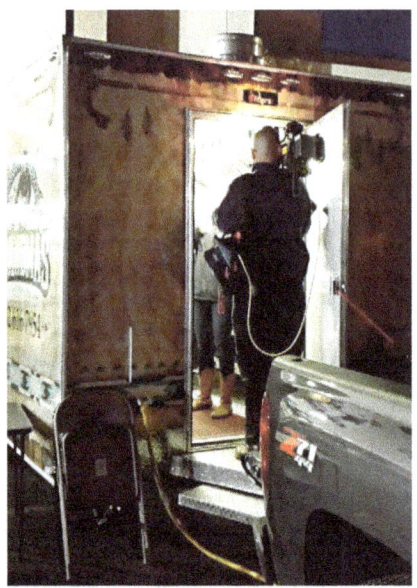

Above and left, videotaping an interview with me that appeared on Arizona Channel 3, 5 and 15 evening news programs.

TV crew filming me making frybread.

Hard at work: Harry on left and Angela on right. *Me tending the dough.* *Manley at work at the grill..*

Hard at work: Me in forefront, my sister Marilyn on right and Angela tending to customers.

Frybread with powdered sugar and cinnamon.

Navajo Taco

Navajo Burger

Navajo pork chop.

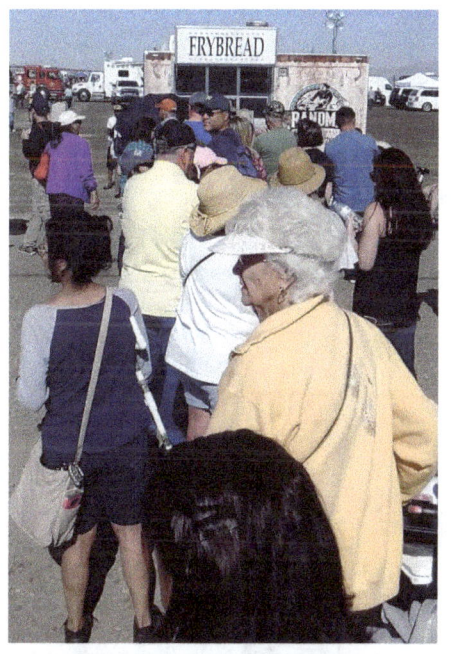

Alicia working in the food trailer.

The line is long for frybread.

Guess which food truck is Newscaster Gina Maravilla's favorite food truck...Grandma's Navajo Frybread!

The coveted "A" rating from the health inspector.

Me (Verna) in a slow moment by our trailer.

The line waiting to order frybread.

Grandma's Frybread trailer in all its glory, left.

Epilogue

The stories contained in this book are the stories that we, the authors, have talked about from time to time over the last 10 or 12 years. We decided to write this book because these are stories that should not be lost with the passage of time, not only by family but by the public at large. While much current thought seems to want to erase history and start over, we firmly believe that our knowledge of history helps us to avoid making the same mistakes that our ancestors did, both personally and as a country.

As we put the book together, it was Verna who provided most of the stories, and Clare and Verna together did the writing. We have succeeded in putting together a book we are proud of. Clare couldn't have written it without Verna's help and Verna wouldn't have written it without Clare's help. We hope you have enjoyed reading it as much as we have enjoyed writing it.

There are lessons subtly entwined in Verna's story that we hope you, the reader, have not missed. Perhaps the most profound is the torment that can be felt by a child when his or her true parentage is kept a secret. Verna has risen above it, but not without soul searching, compromise and some tears.

You should have also learned of the anguish that can be felt by a child who faces abuse in the home, whether spousal, child, or sexual. That is something we don't think an adult who went through this as a child ever recovers from.

Perhaps the most difficult issue entwined in our book is the reservation system itself, a system that was created as a way of getting the indigenous population out of the way so that settlement of the land could occur, and then after settlement was complete was made permanent by Congress with the urging from Commissioner of Indian Affairs John Collier and Secretary of the Interior Harold Ickes under the Franklin D. Roosevelt administration.

Reservation land is owned by the federal government, which deprives the residents of the advantages of sale or mortgage of land and makes it difficult for free enterprise to exist. In fact, it doesn't; it is a communal system. Most people are not aware that residents of Indian reservations are not protected by the United States Constitution, and therefore have no guarantee of freedom of speech, freedom of assembly, and on and on. While that issue is not the main subject of this book, we think the reservation issue needs to be revisited.

We hope you have picked up on the fact that tradition and government are not the same thing and that tradition can be maintained and practiced regardless of where you live. It doesn't matter if you are Irish, German or Navajo, your unique traditions can still be practiced and *should* be practiced or they will be lost. The matter of tradition should not be made a part of government. Tradition, however, should be left to the individual, not forced upon a person like we saw in our story.

Verna is to be commended for having, in spite of the roadblocks put in her path, contributed her talents to society and succeeded in creating a good life for herself and her children. Most of them live off the reservation, and most have established their homes in the Phoenix, Arizona, area. Yet they have not lost the Navajo tradition, each to their own degree.

Verna and I have learned a lot through our research for this book about the history of the Navajo people. We have included a list on page 275 of all the books we read in preparation for writing this book. We would recommend them to anyone whose interest in Navajo history has been aroused, since this book only scratches the surface.

We thoroughly enjoyed putting this book together, and we hope you have enjoyed reading it.

P.S. Since I wrote this epilogue, the U.S. Supreme Court in 2023 seems to have activated that portion of the 14th Amendment to the Constitution that says, "all persons born or naturalized in the United States, are citizens of the United States and of the State wherein they reside. No State shall make or enforce any law which shall abridge the privileges or immunities of citizens of the United States, nor shall any State deprive any person of life, liberty or property, without due process of law, nor deny any person within its jurisdiction the equal protection of the law."

Unfortunately, it will probably take years for this Supreme Court ruling to be fully implemented. I sincerely hope I am wrong.

Clarence Ralph Fitz

Books Read to Prepare for This Book

Kristofic, Jim and Eskeets, Edison *Send a Runner: A Navajo Honors the Long Walk* University of New Mexico Press, Albuquerque, 2011

Schwab, Ron *The Long Walk* Uplands Press, Omaha, NE, 2020

Kristofic, Jim *Medicine Woman: The story of the first Native American Nursing School* University of New Mexico Press, Albuquerque, 2019

Kristofic, Jim and *Send a Runner: A Navajo Honors the Long Walk* Eskeets, Edison University of New Mexico Press, Albuquerque, 2021

Whitney, David C. *The Graphic Story of the American Presidents* J.C. Ferguson Publishing Company, 1973

Zolbrod, Paul G. *Diné bahane': The Navajo Creation Story* University of New Mexico Press, Albuquerque, 1984

Gearhart, Sharon Leslie *Seasons of the Enemies: The Long Walk of the Navajo* Xlibris, 2014

Bial, Raymond *The Long Walk: The Story of Navajo Captivity* Benchmark Books, Tarrytown, NY, 2003

John S. Westerlund *Arizona's War Town Flagstaff, Navajo Ordnance Depot, and World War II* The University of Arizona Press, 2003

Tom Dunlay *Kit Carson and the Indians* University of Nebraska Press, 2000

Chester Nez *Code Talker* Dutton Caliber, 2011

Paul D. Berkowitz *The Case of the Indian Trader* University of New Mexico Press, 2011

Nathan Aaseng *Navajo Code Talkers* Bloomsbury Publishing Plc, 1992

Belle Marvel Brain *The Redemption of the Red Man: An Account of Presbyterian Missions to the North American Indians of the Present Day* The Trow Press, 1904

Doris A. Paul *The Navajo Code Talkers* Dorrance Publishing Co, Inc, 1973

Aurora Hunt *Major General James Henry Carleton 1814 – 1873 Western Frontier Dragoon* The Arthur H. Clark Company

Bernhard Michaelis *The Navajo Treaty 1868* Native Child Dinetah

Introduction by Martin A. Link *The Navajo Treaty – 1868* K C Publications

Prologue references:

The Navajo-U.S. population mortality crossover since the mid-20th century RUSSELL THORNTON University of California at Los Angeles https://eds.p.ebscohost.com/eds/pdfviewer/pdfviewer?vid=10&sid=ba4cf870-cc67-4477-b1b1-a8208baedb97%40redis located on page 5.

https://www.newmexico.org/native-culture/native-communities/navajo-nation-dineh/

https://www.merriam-webster.com/dictionary/half-breed#:~:text=%3A%20the%20offspring%20of%20parents%20of,half%2Dbreed%20adjective%20offensive

Acknowledgments

Clare would like to thank the ladies at the Bosque Redondo Memorial in Fort Sumner and the Memorial itself for substantiating that we were on the right path with the story we were telling in our book.

Clare also would like to thank the ladies at the Canyon de Chelly National Monument Welcome Center for trying valiantly although unsuccessfully to get the video machine to work so he could see the interviews with farmers from the floor of Canyon de Chelly.

Most of all Clare wants to thank the pastor at the Ganado Presbyterian Church for graciously discussing his considerable knowledge of the glory days of the Ganado Mission.

And Clare wants to thank his co-author Verna for trusting him with the stories of her life, some of which were painful for her to remember.

Verna wants to thank her daughter Veronica and her brother Lynn for reading the manuscript while it was in its development and offering advice as well as pointing out errors.

Verna also wants to thank her Dad's family, especially Uncle Joe and Uncle Ellis and brother Lynn for helping her to know more about her Dad.

And Verna wants to thank her family for helping to find the many pictures that appear in the book.

Perhaps most of all, Verna wants to thank her co-author Clare, for persevering over several years to bring the story of her life to print and in the beginning for his suggestion that this book should be written and that we write it.

And finally, both Verna and Clare want to thank Robin at Fideli Publishing for sticking with us during trying times in putting this book together and for her expertise in layout, and for publishing our book.

Other Books by Clare Fitz

"...and the Mille Lacs who have no reservation..."
Fideli Publishing, Inc., 2016

The Pendulum...from Indian Removal to buying Mille Lacs
Fideli Publishing, Inc., 2020

Ralph
Fideli Publishing, Inc, 2022

www.ingramcontent.com/pod-product-compliance
Lightning Source LLC
Chambersburg PA
CBHW070910120626

46546CB00001B/206